# THE
## traditional
# AGA
## Cookery BOOK

First published in 1994 by Absolute Press, Scarborough House, 29 James Street West, Bath, BA1 2BT.
Tel: 01225 316013 Fax: 01225 445836 email: sales@absolutepress.demon.co.uk

Reprinted 1995 (three times)
Reprinted 1996 (three times)
Reprinted 1997 (twice)
Reprinted 1998 (twice)
Reprinted 2000
Reprinted 2002

Aga-Rayburn is a trading name of Glynwed Consumer Products Ltd.

ISBN 0 948230 78 9

Cover and text Design by Ian Middleton
Cover and text illustrations by Caroline Nisbett

Printed by The Cromwell Press, Trowbridge, Wiltshire
Covers printed by Devenish and Co. Bath

# THE
# traditional
# AGA
# Cookery BOOK

## Louise Walker

ABSOLUTE PRESS

# CONTENTS

# GENERAL
# INTRODUCTION

## CONVERSION CHART

This is the metric/imperial conversion chart that I have used. Do keep to either metric or imperial measures throughout the whole recipe; mixing the two can lead to all kinds of problems. Eggs used in testing have been size 3. Tablespoon and teaspoon measures have been flat unless otherwise stated.
Flour is always plain unless stated.

### *Conversion Table*

| | |
|---|---|
| 1 oz | 25g |
| 2 oz | 50g |
| 3 oz | 75g |
| 4 oz | 100g |
| 5 oz | 150g |
| 6 oz | 175g |
| 7 oz | 200g |
| 8 oz | 225g |
| 9 oz | 250g |
| 10 oz | 275g |
| 11 oz | 300g |
| 12 oz | 350g |
| 13 oz | 375g |
| 14 oz | 400g |
| 15 oz | 425g |
| 16 oz (1 lb) | 450g |
| 2lbs | 1kg |
| | |
| 1 tsp | 5ml |
| 1 tbsp | 15ml |
| 1/4 pint | 150ml |
| 1/2 pint | 300ml |
| 3/4 pint | 450ml |
| 1 pint | 600ml |
| 2 pints | 1 litre |
| | |
| 8 inch tin | 20cm tin |

# GENERAL
# INTRODUCTION

...................................................

This book is intended as a useful handbook for Aga owners. It cannot be a definitive recipe book, but I have tried to cover all the basic topics that crop up when teaching new and experienced Aga owners how to use their Aga to full effect. I hope it will be a constant reference point and a basis for using other new and well tried recipes with confidence.

I know from the demonstrating and workshop sessions I run, that there are two types of Aga owner: those who choose to put an Aga into their homes and those who inherit an Aga when they move house. The former have either been brought up with an Aga, or they have had the opportunity to observe the multitude of benefits bestowed by the presence of an Aga. The latter are often terrified by the great monster in the kitchen but, after only a few months, the fear has gone and they are quite converted.

We all love the constant warmth, the instant oven – great to pop a meal into at the end of a busy shopping trip – the area to dry clothes and air the ironing. My sons have to have a ritual lean on the Aga before they start the day!

I keep my Aga on all year round. When the weather is hot, I open the doors and windows of the kitchen and if the weather is really sizzling, who wants to be in the kitchen cooking anyway? If salads will not do, I can usually find something to defrost from the freezer and then I need the Aga to refresh the food or thaw it out.

I have yet to find an Aga owner, new or old, who would change to another cooker, let alone give up all those other conveniences. The most popular selling Agas at the moment are gas-fired. However, not so long ago solid fuel was the popular fuel for Agas and some people still think that Agas can only be properly run on solid fuel. In fact many other fuels can be used: electricity, liquid propane gas and oil.

The solid fuel Agas are the most complicated to run and, if yours is one of those, your own experience will tell you how to fuel it for the particular cooking task in hand. Fortunately this experience does not take long to acquire. As with all Agas, keep the lids down as much as possible; some people open the vent door to give

an extra boost of heat during cooking. Agas converted from solid fuel to oil or gas often have "personality" differences. For example the simmering oven may be too cool or too warm for some recipes. These personality differences are in fact typical of all Agas. They all run differently because they are made individually and are sited and fuelled differently.

Like all new kitchen appliances, it takes time to get to know your Aga; perhaps this is the secret of the great Aga-owners' loyalty – it becomes a personality in the kitchen. However, all this does mean that writing recipes for an Aga can in no way be regarded as an "exact science". Almost everything should be treated as guidelines. I hope that the recipes in this book will give you ideas on the efficient use of your Aga and on its range of capabilities. You can then go on to experiment confidently with other recipes.

# LOOKING AFTER YOUR AGA

Keep an eye on the heat indicator on the front of the Aga: the mercury should be on the black line. If I am doing a lot of cooking or entertaining, at Christmas time, for example, I turn my Aga up a little for an extra boost of heat. Should the mercury reach the red mark, turn the Aga down immediately. If the Aga continues to overheat, turn it off and call the Aga engineer.

If you are used to the chore of cleaning a gas or electric cooker, you will love the simplicity of keeping the Aga clean. Mine gets a thorough clean just once a year, when it is switched off for servicing; mine is gas-fired, an oil-fired one needs 6-monthly servicing. The night before servicing I switch off the Aga completely. After the breakfast is cleared away I set to on the cleaning and try to do as much as possible before the engineer arrives. Remove everything possible; the oven shelves and the doors which simply lift off. Brush out all the carbon deposits from the ovens. Anything still sticky on the floor of the oven can be removed with a wooden spatula, and the remains left to carbonise.

Clean the lids of the boiling and simmering plates, and round the inside of the oven door frames, with a warm soapy cloth and a paste cleaner such as Astonish. **Never** be tempted to use a wire wool pad or a tough abrasive. Some elbow grease may be needed, but you will be surprised how much dirt will

come off. Rinse off with a clean cloth and buff up. Clean the oven shelves in a sink of soapy water and more Astonish if needed. Replace. Wipe round the doors and clean the inside of the roasting and baking oven doors if necessary. The other doors will probably not get dirty. If you are concerned about the state of the seals remember to get the engineer to check them. Return all the bits and pieces to their places and give the whole Aga a wipe down and buff up. I know some people who even polish their Agas occasionally! Other than the annual clean try to wipe up any spills as they occur, and wipe off any other crumbs, dust and so on daily. I find a lot of dust on my Aga, partly due to all the laundry put to dry or air above it.

# POTS, PANS AND ACCESSORIES

Many people worry about their saucepans when they have a new Aga. New pans purchased with an Aga will last a lifetime if they are looked after, because there is no warping of the bases due to the large, even-heat area. However, it isn't always necessary to rush out and buy new pans. Think carefully about what you need and buy one or two at a time.

If you have existing pans there are two ways of testing their suitability for the Aga. Turn the pan upside down and put a ruler or something with a straight edge across the base. If daylight shows through, the pan will not work efficiently. Alternatively, half fill the pan with water and put on the boiling plate to boil. If only a poor contact is being made, the water will not boil. Beware – even toast crumbs on the plate can have the same effect. A good, heavy-based pan is best. The size, shape and metal varies, so choose according to your personal needs and preferences. Pans that go on the hot plates and in the oven are very useful. The Aga showroom will have a good range to show you.

A kettle is essential, but the shape and style are your own personal preference. Choose a heavy base and ask if you can do a water pouring test in the showroom or shop so that you know that the kettle suits you.

The Aga roasting tins are useful because they fit the runners of the ovens and can be used as extra shelves. I find two small tins most useful, putting meat to roast in one tin and vegetables in another, or if I need only half a shelf I use one roasting tin. The roasting rack for one tin is handy to use when roasting fatty meat, or for grilling bacon, sausages and chops.

You will use oven-proof dishes quite a lot, because so much cooking is done in the ovens. I find pans and casseroles that can be used on the top plates AND in the oven especially useful but wooden or plastic "handles" like those on the Agaluxe range cannot be used in the roasting oven, and in time wooden handles will dry out and come apart. Cast iron pans and dishes are useful for their multi-purpose use, but they can be heavy to lift.

# COOKING WITH THE AGA

The Aga works on the basis of stored heat, so the aim with all cooking is to allow as little heat loss as possible. As soon as the boiling plate or simmering plate lids are lifted, heat will be lost, so use the ovens as much as possible, and yes it is possible to cook Sunday lunch for a houseful and for everyone to have a bath in the morning as well!

Frying, steaming and grilling can be done in the oven, while toast is made using the "tennis racket" under the closed lid of the boiling plate.

The hot plates or cooking plates are the same on both the 2-oven and 4-oven Aga models. To maintain heat, the heavy insulated lids are kept down when the plate is not in use. The shiny lids are slightly domed. Do not be tempted to put the kettle or other pots and pans on the top without using a protective pad: once scratched always scratched. The boiling plate is on the left. It sits directly over the boiler, and will boil a kettle of water with remarkable speed, boil pasta and vegetables, make good toast and stir-fry brilliantly. The simmering plate is on the right. I find mine cooks rather faster than a simmer, but it is brilliant for steaming vegetables, making sauces, heating milk, frying and general warming through. This plate is also used as a griddle for making Scotch pancakes, Welsh cakes and oatcakes. You can melt chocolate, butter and syrups and warm milk simply by standing the food in a bowl or pan, on top of the Aga: there's no danger of overheating. Always remember – as soon as cooking is finished put the lids down so that heat level is restored.

The ovens, which look so small from the outside, are very spacious inside. Two small roasting tins will go in back-to-back. Aga roasting tins are designed to fit exactly so that they will slide on the runners without the use of the oven shelf. The new Agas are supplied with one small roasting tin with a rack to fit, and a large roasting tin and rack. The larger rack makes a useful cooling rack when you are doing a lot of baking. Two oven shelves with useful anti-tilt devices are also

supplied. If you have the opportunity, try sliding the shelves in and out of the oven before the Aga is fired up. They are easy to use once you have the knack, but difficult to manage when hot if you have not tried it before. I know one couple who spent a whole day trying to get their shelves out! The mysterious cold plain shelf is also supplied. This fits the runners and can be used as an oven shelf or a baking tray. However, for the 2-oven Aga, it should be kept out of the oven, somewhere cool, so that it can be used to diffuse the heat above food cooking in the roasting oven. I met one lady, an Aga owner for 30 years, who did not know what the cold plain shelf was really for. No wonder she thought my demonstration was a revelation! More details on how to use this shelf will be found in the recipes, especially those for cake making.

The 4-oven Aga has a baking oven which is at a permanently moderate heat, ideal for cakes, biscuits and puddings. The simmering oven on both models can be used for cooking food slowly, and even overnight. Most foods need to be pre-heated before cooking in this oven, either on the simmering or boiling plate or in the roasting oven. There are one or two exceptions, for example meringues and porridge. The 2-oven Aga simmering oven can be used for warming plates, whereas the 4-oven Aga has a plate warming oven, where plates will keep warm without risk of cracking.

# TIPS AND USES FOR THE AGA

One of the best tips I was given when my Aga was new was "buy a timer you can carry around with you"! I now know why. There are no smells from the Aga, so it is easy to forget. I think all Aga owners have opened the oven and thought, "what WAS that lump of charcoal?" Those yellow sticky note pads are useful – reminders on the breakfast table to "remember porridge" or "remember stock/Christmas cakes/puddings", are invaluable. I have been known to put a reminder "remember casserole" on my pillow, so that I remove it before going to bed!

Dry baking tins and awkwardly shaped cooking utensils on top of the Aga – there are no excuses for rusty tins.

Pastry cases for quiches do not need to be baked blind. Simply cook them directly on the floor of the roasting oven for a crisp base. It is safe to use porcelain, glass and metal flan dishes.

Stand mugs of tea or coffee on top of the Aga to keep warm when the telephone rings.

To defrost cakes or bread, stand them on top of the simmering plate lid or place them in the simmering oven.

Dry your washing on top of the simmering plate lid – the boiling plate is too hot. Spin the items to be dried, smooth out any creases and lay on the lid: no ironing needed! Hang towels or sheets over the chrome rail – just take care not to cover the air vents on the control box door.

If your kitchen ceiling is high enough, a kitchen maid above the Aga is useful for drying washing. Hang flowers to dry on the ends so that it does not look too utilitarian.

Rugby boots washed of all their mud, and washed trainers, can be hung by their laces on the chrome rail to dry.

Shoes wet from winter rain should be stuffed full with newspaper and dried in front of the Aga – the gentle heat will not spoil the leather.

When the snow comes, the Aga heat is busy not just producing hot food but drying snowy gloves and socks, as well as warming coats and hats and boots.

Finally, a word about oven gloves. Go for the long Aga gauntlets to avoid burnt arms reaching to the back of the oven to get that elusive dish or potato. I was once told a story by a long-time Aga owner of a 1940's war-time dinner party. My story-teller was at a military dinner and was placed next to a smart and slightly superior lady. Gloves (always worn in those days) were removed and dinner started. My story-teller leaned towards the smart lady and said, "I see you are an Aga owner." Much fluster followed, perhaps she thought she smelt of cooking. Anyway, all was soon revealed; "I can tell by the burn marks up your arms!" said the story-teller. "Look at mine." A relaxed evening followed in an exchange of Aga stories.

# 20 QUESTIONS ANSWERED

......................................................

**1. DO I REALLY NEED ANOTHER COOKER FOR BAKING CAKES AND BISCUITS?**

No. With the 2-oven Aga, biscuits and cakes can easily be baked without burning by using the cold plain shelf. Larger cakes can be baked in the cake baker. See the section on cakes and biscuits for more detail. Of course the 4-oven Aga has a baking oven ideally suited for baking cakes and biscuits of all types.

**2. DO I NEED TO BUY A WHOLE SET OF PANS TO GO WITH MY NEW AGA?**

Take your time about choosing pans. It is important that they have a ground base for making good contact with the boiling and simmering plates. Each family has different needs for shapes, sizes of pans, so look at the range available for use with an Aga before choosing. See the General Introduction section on Pots ,Pans and Accessories for more detail.

**3. THERE IS NO GRILL ON THE AGA, HOW WILL I GRILL CHOPS AND BROWN FOOD? DO I HAVE TO RETURN TO FRYING?**

A grill isn't needed on the Aga because food put in the highest position of the roasting oven will brown in the same way as with a grill. Either place the oven shelf on the highest runner possible, or use the roasting tin hung on the top set of runners. This tin is just like a grill pan if the rack is fitted inside. Chops and sausages cook in just the same way as with a grill, without the mess and with a more moist result!

Frying can be done on the floor of the roasting oven, should you wish to cook that way. The cast-iron Aga pans work very well on the floor of the oven, as well as on the hot plates.

**4. ALL MY FRIENDS TELL ME THAT IT IS EASY TO RUN OUT OF HEAT. WILL I MANAGE TO COOK A MEAL FOR A CROWD?**

Yes, easily. Heat is lost as soon as the lids are lifted and so, to prevent heat loss and filling the kitchen with steam and smells, cook as much as possible

in the oven. Virtually everything can be cooked in the oven.

5. **HOW CAN I COOK MASSES OF VEGETABLES TO GO WITH THE SUNDAY ROAST WITHOUT THE TEMPERATURE DROPPING?**
All root vegetables can be cooked in the oven, thus saving heat. Place the vegetables in a saucepan with salt to taste and half covered with water. Stand on the boiling plate, cover with a lid and bring to the boil. Boil for 1-2 minutes. If time is short leave the water in the pan and transfer directly to the simmering oven, alternatively if preparing well in advance, drain the water off and transfer, in the hot saucepan, to the simmering oven.

Green vegetables are best cooked quickly, so plunge into fast-boiling, salted water for the minimum cooking time to give crisp, bright vegetables – alternatively steam the vegetables.

6. **CAN I STILL USE MY WOK? STIR-FRYING IS SUCH A PART OF MY COOKING THESE DAYS.**
Woks rely on a good heat source up the side of the pan so that food can be cooked all over the surface of the wok. This heating is not satisfactory on the Aga boiling plate; however I find a large, deep frying pan almost the size of the hot plate is perfect for stir-frying.

7. **MUST I USE AGA RECIPES ONLY OR CAN I ADAPT MY FAVOURITES? I DON'T FEEL VERY CONFIDENT.**
Any recipe can be used, but confidence is the key to successful use of the Aga. Like any new piece of kitchen equipment, take time to read the recipe/instruction books, be prepared for some mistakes and experiment. The recipes in the book have been chosen to illustrate the basic methods needed when using the Aga. As a guideline: the left-hand plate is for boiling, stir-frying and rapid cooking; the right-hand plate is for simmering, gently frying, making sauces, heating milk; the roasting oven is very hot, and the nearer the top the hotter the oven; the baking oven is a more moderate heat – on the 4-oven Aga only; the simmering oven is cooler and often needs food pre-heating before cooking.

Giving actual temperatures would be misleading as every Aga is different, especially the temperature of the simmering oven. Converted Agas often have very cool simmering ovens suitable just for plate warming.

8. **SHOULD I TURN THE AGA OFF WHEN I GO AWAY FOR THE WEEKEND?**

No. For a weekend the Aga is happy left at the usual setting, or if the weather is very hot the Aga can be turned down a point or two.

9. **FOR HOLIDAY TIME CAN I LEAVE THE AGA RUNNING?**

For a longer time away it is best to turn the Aga down very low or leave the pilot position. This will allow a quick return to temperature when the holiday ends.

10. **IS IT NECESSARY TO HAVE MY AGA SERVICED REGULARLY?**

Yes. For efficient safe running have the Aga serviced annually – except oil Agas, which should be serviced every six months. When the Aga is turned off it is a good time to give the Aga a good clean. This is the time to bring out the old electric kettle and toaster!

11. **MERINGUES MADE IN THE AGA HAVE A WONDERFUL REPUTATION, BUT MINE ARE STICKY AND WET. WHAT AM I DOING WRONG?**

Meringues can be tricky and advice difficult. Firstly, when making the meringues the sugar must be whisked in slowly, I only whisk in 1 teaspoonful at a time. Then spoon onto a plain shelf, lined with rice paper, silicone paper or Bake-o-Glide.

Slide the tray into the centre of the simmering oven, this is where timing is difficult because ovens vary. I cook my meringues for about 4 hours; if they are not as dry as I like I leave them in but with the oven door slightly open. The meringues will dry but not colour. I have actually forgotton one batch and left them in over 48 hours – to no harm.

12. **I HAVE AN AGA CONVERTED FROM SOLID FUEL TO OIL. I FIND THE ROASTING OVEN VERY HOT, EVEN WHEN TURNED LOW. HOW CAN I REGULATE IT FOR COOKING?**

Knowing that your Aga is hot compared with other Agas, you will need to allow shorter cooking time for roasts etc., and use a lower shelf, because the top of the oven is always hottest. Use the cold shelf, not just for cake and biscuit making, but to cut down heat for other foods. Use the cake baker to form an insulating jacket, or even put a dish inside an old silvery biscuit tin.

**13. WHEN I COOK FISH FOR A MAIN COURSE CAN I STILL COOK THE PUDDING AT THE SAME TIME OR WILL THE FISH TAINT THE PUDDING?**

Because the Aga has a proper flue, and the air is not being circulated in the oven then there will be no overlap of flavours.

**14. IF I CAN'T SMELL FOOD COOKING IN THE OVENS, HOW DO I STOP FOOD BURNING?**

Equip yourself with a timer, preferably one that is either very loud so you can leave the kitchen, or one to carry round. I have seen a light fixed over Agas that are switched on when food goes in the oven. I also use little sticky Post-it labels which I put on the breakfast table to remind me of porridge.

**15. HOW DO I CLEAN THE AGA WHEN IT IS HOT ALL THE TIME?**

As the Aga is hot all the time, food spills and splashes will carbonise on the hotplates and in the oven and can be brushed off with a wire brush. Wipe over the vitreous enamel as soon as spills occur, this stops any acid damage to the enamel. The enamelled surface can be cleaned safely with Astonish paste on a damp cloth, then rinsed and buffed up.

**16. CAN I DRY MY WASHING ON MY AGA?**

Yes. There are two points to be careful about. Do not cover any air vents in doors, so that burning of the fuel can continue properly balanced and don't put laundry on the boiling plate lid as it is hot enough to scorch. Hang laundry on a clothes-horse or a kitchen maid overnight or when you are out. Fold sheets etc. and put on the simmering plate lid to dry or air. They will iron themselves. Don't forget baking tins as well — they can be put to dry so they won't rust during storage.

**17. THE OVENS SEEM VERY SMALL, I DON'T GET EVERYTHING IN I NEED.**

The difference with the Aga oven and conventional gas or electric ovens is that the whole space can be used as there are no hot elements or burners. So put tins, dishes etc. right to the back and the sides, and of course the floor can be used, for example cooking pastry to get a crisp base, frying fish or eggs. The ovens are deep, but remember the shelves can easily be pulled forward to get at things and the Aga gauntlets can be used.

18. **I LIKE TO MAKE BREAD. WHERE SHOULD I STAND THE DOUGH TO RISE?**

The Aga is perfect for bread-making. The warm, even heat is always to hand for rising. Here are a few tips. Warm the flour at the back of the Aga. When the dough is made, put it to rise on top or near the Aga. If you stand the bowl or baking sheet on the Aga remember to use a folded tea-towel or trivet. This not only protects the surface from scratching but stops the dough getting too hot and 'cooking'. Before baking make sure the oven is well up to temperature, as bread needs to be baked in a hot oven.

19. **MY FAMILY COME IN AT ALL DIFFERENT TIMES FOR MEALS. CAN I KEEP FOOD HOT ON THE AGA OR SHOULD I JUST RE-HEAT IT IN MY MICRO-WAVE?**

Food will keep hot and moist in the simmering oven for about an hour without spoiling. Drain rice and vegetables and put in serving dishes, cover and keep warm ready to serve. Sauces keep hot very well if made in advance also.

20. **FRIENDS TALK ABOUT 'THE AGA CAKE BAKER'. WHAT IS IT?**

This mysterious object is only needed by 2 oven Aga owners as those with a 4-oven Aga have an oven specially designed to allow a deep cake to cook through without being burnt on the outside.

The pan of the cake baker is heated in the roasting oven while the cake is being made. The cake mixture is then put in the chosen tin. The tin is fixed into the trivet and this is then put into the hot cake baker. This set is returned to the roasting oven and the cake is baked for 1-2 hours according to type, size etc. Remove from the baker at the end of cooking and cool in the normal way. The pan of the cake baker can be used as a good-sized saucepan which can be used in all areas of the Aga.

# BASIC AGA TECHNIQUES

## FISH

Cooking fish in the Aga is so easy and cuts out fishy smells! The variety of fish available is increasing all the time, so experiment with different fish and different cooking methods. I have given approximate cooking times, but this will depend upon the size and thickness of the fish. Try not to overcook, as this gives dry, stringy, tasteless fish.

### POACHING FISH
Place the fish in a roasting tin, cover with water, wine or milk, salt, pepper and a bayleaf. Cover loosely with foil and hang the tin on the third set of runners from the top for 15-20 minutes.

### POACHING WHOLE LARGE FISH e.g. SALMON
Clean the fish. Sprinkle with salt if desired, and wrap in buttered foil. Lift the parcel into the large roasting tin, pour boiling water into the tin to come half-way up the fish. Hang on the second set of runners from the top of the roasting oven. Cook for 10 minutes per lb (450g), turning the fish half-way through cooking. Remove it from the oven and allow it to cool. Serve warm or remove the skin when cold.

### FRIED FISH
Wash and dry the fish. If required, coat it with either seasoned flour, batter, oatmeal or egg and fresh breadcrumbs. Put enough cooking oil into the roasting tin to coat the base. Put the tin on the floor of the roasting oven and heat until hazing. Add the fish and continue to cook on the floor of the oven. Turn the fish half-way through the cooking time.

### GRILLED FISH
Lay fish cutlets in a roasting tin, brush with oil and seasoning. Hang the tin on the highest set of runners and grill, turning over half-way through the cooking time. It sometimes rings the changes to marinade the fish for half an hour and grill on the rack of the roasting tin, basting or brushing with a little more marinade part way through cooking. This will give a more charred appearance and taste.

# ROASTING MEAT

Meat roasted in the Aga will be moist and flavoursome, with only a smearing of extra fat needed to start the cooking. Season as you prefer with salt, pepper, or fresh herbs. If the meat is to be stuffed, do this and then weigh it to calculate cooking times. There are two methods of roasting using the Aga. The Quick Roasting Method is the more traditional method, used for more tender cuts of meat. The Slow Roasting Method is best for less fine cuts of meat.

## QUICK ROASTING METHOD

Season the meat and put it in the Aga roasting tin. Stand it on the rack, if you prefer. Hang the tin on the bottom set of runners of the roasting oven for the calculated time. Baste with hot fat periodically. The shape of the joint will also affect the cooking time – a long narrow joint will not take so long as a short, fat joint. When the meat is cooked, allow the joint to rest in the simmering oven for 15 minutes before carving. This is a useful time to make gravy and cook last-minute vegetables.

## SLOW ROASTING METHOD

Season and prepare the meat as above. Put the roasting tin into the roasting oven on the bottom set of runners for 30 minutes or until the meat is browning and getting hot. Transfer to the bottom set of runners of the simmering oven and cook for twice the time calculated for the Quick Roasting Method.

## TIMES FOR ROASTING:

| | |
|---|---|
| Roast Beef: | |
| rare | 10 minutes per lb/450g plus 10 minutes |
| medium | 15 minutes per lb/450g plus 15 minutes |
| well done | 20 minutes per lb/450g plus 20 minutes |
| Fillet: | 10 minutes per lb/450g plus 10 minutes |
| | |
| Roast Pork: | 30 minutes per lb/450g plus 30 minutes |
| | |
| Lamb: | |
| pink | 15 minutes per lb/450g plus 15 minutes |
| medium | 20 minutes per lb/450g plus 20 minutes |
| | |
| Veal: | 20 minutes per lb/450g plus 20 minutes |

# ROASTING POULTRY AND GAME

Roast poultry and game from the Aga will produce crisp skin on the outside of moist tender flesh. Most poultry is cooked in the roasting oven by the normal method, but a large turkey can be cooked in the simmering oven, useful when cooking for a crowd, or to take the rush and bustle from Christmas morning. Nowadays it is not considered safe to stuff poultry before roasting, though the neck end of turkey can still be filled if not the cavity. Always allow extra cooking time for this stuffing.

Smear the bird with a little butter. Put bacon rashers over the breast if liked. Stand on the trivet in the roasting tin. Put lemon or herbs in the body cavity if liked. Cover with a little foil − not tightly or this will slow the cooking time. Hang the tin on the lowest set of runners of the roasting oven for the following times. Remove the foil for the last 15 minutes to allow browning.

### ROASTING TIMES
(N.B: ensure that oven is up to correct temperature before roasting.)

| Bird | Weight | Approximate cooking times |
| --- | --- | --- |
| Chicken | 2lb/900g | 45-50 minutes |
| | 3lb/1.5kg | 1 hour |
| | 4lb/1.75kg | 1$^1/_2$ hours |
| | 5lb/2.25kg | 1$^3/_4$ hours |
| Turkey | Weigh the bird after stuffing and allow 15 minutes per 450g/1lb + 15 minutes. Remove from oven and leave for 30 minutes to allow the flesh to firm up. | |
| Duck | | 1-1$^1/_2$ hours |
| Goose | | 1$^1/_2$ − 2 hours |
| Grouse | | 30-35 minutes |
| Pigeon | | 20-35 minutes |
| Partridge | | 30-35 minutes |

| Pheasant | 45-50 minutes |
|---|---|
| Quail | 15 minutes |
| Snipe | 15 minutes |
| Woodcock | 15 minutes |

To test if cooked, pierce the thickest part of the thigh with a fine skewer, and if the juices run clear the bird is cooked. Allow the bird to rest in the simmering oven whilst making gravy from the skimmed cooking juices.

# SLOW ROASTING OF TURKEY

Prepare the turkey in the usual way, stand on the rack in the roasting tin. Cover loosely with foil and slide onto the floor of the simmering oven for the following length of time:

| 0-10lb/3.5-4.5kg | about 9-10 hours |
|---|---|
| 11-15lb/5-7.25kg | about 11-12 hours |
| 16-22lb/7.5-10kg | about 13-14 hours |

Remove the foil and pop into the roasting oven for the last 15 minutes of cooking time to crisp the skin. Test in the usual way.

# BOILED BACON AND GAMMON JOINTS

Cooking a whole piece of ham in the Aga is so easy and gives a moist joint, perfect for slicing. I even cook ham for friends because they love the moistness, and really it takes very little effort.

Soak the joint in water for 2-3 hours to remove any saltiness. Put a rack or an old saucer in the bottom of a suitably sized pan. Put the joint on top and pour

in enough cold water to come 2–3 inches up the side of the pan. Cover. Stand on the simmering plate and bring slowly to the boil, then simmer for 30 minutes. Transfer the joint to the floor of the simmering oven for the following times:

| | |
|---|---|
| 2 – 3 lb/900g – 1.5kg | 2¹/₂ hours |
| 4 – 5 lb/1.75 – 2.25kg | 3 hours |
| 6 – 7 lb/2.75 – 3 kg | 3¹/₂ hours |
| 8 – 9 lb/3.5 – 4 kg | 4¹/₂ hours |
| 10 – 11 lb/4.5 – 5kg | 5¹/₂ hours |
| 12 – 13 lb/5.5 – 6kg | 6¹/₂ hours |
| 14 – 15 lb/6.5 – 6.75kg | 7¹/₂ hours |
| 16 lb/7.25kg and over | overnight |

Remove from the oven and the pan. Cool a little to handle. Strip off the skin and score the fat. Mix together a glaze of mustard and honey and spread over the surface. Stud with cloves if liked. Stand in a roasting tin with the glazing uppermost and cover the meat with foil. Hang the tin so that the meat is fairly near the top of the roasting oven and bake for 10-20 minutes, until a golden glaze has formed. Watch it closely, it may burn! Serve hot or cold.

## STOCKS

Home-made stocks are easy to make in the Aga and they certainly taste better than the cubes. If you make a large pot full, freeze in quantities that are most useful: 1 pint/600ml for soups, ¹/₂ pints/300ml for gravies etc.

### BEEF, LAMB, CHICKEN, GAME

Place the bones of the chosen meat in a large saucepan. Add a selection of flavouring vegetables, e.g. onions, carrots, celery, washed and chopped, but not necessarily peeled. Add some peppercorns and a bouquet garni. Cover with cold water and put on a lid. Place pan on the boiling plate and bring to the boil. Transfer to the simmering plate, and simmer for 10 minutes. Transfer to the simmering oven and leave for 12 hours or overnight. Remove from the oven, cool and skim off excess fat. Strain through a sieve and either store in the fridge for immediate use, or freeze. For a darker stock, roast the bones in a roasting tin on the bottom set of runners of the roasting oven for 45 minutes before proceeding as above.

### VEGETABLE STOCK

Wash and chop a selection of vegetables, for example onions, carrots, leeks,

celery, turnips, broccoli. Place them in a large pan and cover with water. Add a few peppercorns and a bouquet garni of whatever fresh herbs are to hand. Bring to the boil on the boiling plate, move to the simmering plate and simmer for 10 minutes. Transfer to the simmering oven and leave for 3-4 hours. Remove and strain through a sieve. Discard the now flavourless vegetables. Pack and freeze the cold stock, or store in the fridge for immediate use.

### FISH STOCK

Place a selection of bones from unsmoked fish in a saucepan. Add washed and roughly chopped vegetables like carrots and onions, a few peppercorns and a bouquet garni. Cover with fresh, cold water. Bring to the boil on the boiling plate, move to the simmering plate and simmer for 10 minutes. Transfer to the simmering oven and cook for 1 hour. Remove from the oven, strain through a sieve and store the cold stock in the fridge for 2 days or the freezer for no more than 2 months.

## BOILED POTATOES AND OTHER ROOT VEGETABLES

Potatoes, along with other root vegetables, are best cooked in the simmering oven. This both conserves the stored heat in the Aga and prevents the kitchen filling with steam. You will need to use a pan that can be used on the boiling plate and in the simmering oven, so no wooden handles. Do not be tempted to transfer the potatoes to a cold serving dish partway through cooking – the entire heat of the pan, water and vegetables is needed for successful cooking.

Wash and prepare the potatoes in the usual way. Cut them to an even size. Place in the pan, add salt to taste, cover with cold water. Put on lid and bring to the boil on the boiling plate. When boiling well, transfer to the simmering oven. It is difficult to give timings, the length of cooking time will depend upon the type of potato and the size of them. Allow 30 minutes and then test. Small new potatoes and small pieces of root vegetable will take about 20 minutes. Drain the vegetables, toss in butter if liked, and serve or return to the pan and the oven to keep warm.

## ROASTING VEGETABLES

Roast vegetables are always a great favourite. I know that it is fashionably healthy to eat baked potatoes instead of roast, and steamed instead of roast parsnips, but nothing beats roast vegetables with roast meat for a special treat.

Peel and cut the vegetables to an even size. Boil for one minute in salted water, then drain thoroughly. While the vegetables are draining and drying, put some cooking oil, lard or dripping into the roasting tin. Slide into the roasting oven on the second set of runners from the top. When the fat is hot, tip in the dry vegetables, toss them in the fat and return to the oven. If you are also roasting meat it may be necessary to juggle the tins during cooking. Cooking near the top will give an evenly cooked, crispy vegetable. Putting on the floor of the oven will crisp the bottom of the vegetables well. They can be put into the top of the baking oven in the 4 oven Aga but may need to be finally crisped in the top of the roasting oven. Vegetables take about 1 hour to roast. If the vegetables are put around the meat they may take longer and are often not so crispy, but they do taste wonderful!

# COOKING RICE

A lot of people seem to have trouble cooking rice. Cooked in the simmering oven of the Aga, it is very simple and it can be kept hot without spoiling if you want to cook it slightly in advance. This is the basic method for cooking rice. Adjust the quantities to suit your needs. Use a pan that will be happy on the boiling plate and in the simmering oven.

*1 cup rice*
*1½ cups water*
*a good pinch of salt*

Wash the rice in a sieve, with cold, running water. Put in the saucepan. Add salt and water and put on the lid.

Bring to the boil on the boiling plate. When boiling, transfer the pan to the floor of the simmering oven.

Cook for the appropriate time. The times I have given produce a cooked, non-soggy rice. If you like rice a little more cooked, then leave it in the oven a little longer.

Remove the pan from the oven and drain the rice through a sieve — some rice will have absorbed all the water. If liked, rinse with boiling water and serve. Alternatively, if you want to keep the rice hot, return to the pan and stir in a small knob of butter. Cover and return to the simmering oven until required.

## COOKING TIMES:

| | |
|---|---|
| White long-grain rice | 12 minutes |
| Brown long-grain rice | 20 minutes |
| Basmati rice | 12 minutes |

# COOKING PASTA

Pasta needs a fast boil when cooking to prevent it sticking together. Try to use a pan that is deeper than its width. Half fill with water, add salt to taste, put the lid on and bring to the boil on the boiling plate. Add the pasta, fresh or dried, cover and bring back to the boil – this will not take long. Remove the lid and start timing according to the packet instructions. It may be necessary to move the pan half-on, half-off the boiling plate to prevent the water boiling over, but try to keep the water and pasta moving. When *al dente*, drain through a colander, return to the pan and toss in a little oil or butter to prevent sticking. Serve straight away with a chosen sauce.

# DRIED BEANS AND PEAS

The range of dried beans available in the shops gives a whole host of flavours, colours and textures for cooking. The beans and other grains can be used for vegetarian cooking or to make meat dishes go further or just to add variety. Lentils do not need soaking before cooking, just washing and picking over. All the other pulses need to be washed, picked over and left to soak for 8-12 hours or overnight – so some forethought is necessary.

Measure out the pulses required, wash well and pick over to remove any grit. Place in a bowl and cover with cold water. Put aside to soak.

Drain the liquid from the beans. Place in a saucepan, cover with cold water and bring to the boil. Boil rapidly for 10 minutes – to prevent boiling over use a large pan and no lid at this stage. After 10 minutes rapid boil, cover and transfer to the simmering oven until tender, 1-3 hours. The length of time depends upon the type and age of the bean. Experience will be your best judge. When cooked, use as per recipe.

# BREAKFASTS

These days most families do not eat a traditional English breakfast on a daily basis, but it is lovely at weekends and holiday-time, when there is time to linger. Breakfast is so simple to cook in the Aga. The only part I do on the top is to boil the kettle for tea and to make the toast, unless I am serving unsweetened Scotch pancakes with the bacon, and then I make those on the simmering plate.

I give an outline for cooking sausages, bacon, tomato and egg, but of course you can add in any extras such as black puddings, scrambled eggs, mushrooms and kidneys. You will need the roasting tin, choose the large or small depending upon the quantity you are cooking for. Lay into the slightly greased roasting tin the sausages, or the thickest food that takes the most cooking. Slide the tin onto the top set of runners in the roasting oven. Cook the sausages for about 10 minutes until golden brown and sizzling. Remove the tin from the oven and lay in the bacon rashers and the tomatoes, cut in half with a cross cut in the middle to help cooking.

Turn over the sausages and return to the oven, again at the top. Cook for a further 10 minutes, this time will depend upon how you like your bacon cooked and the

thickness of the rashers. Remove the sausages to a warm plate and into the simmering oven, also the tomato and bacon if cooked to your preference. If not, leave in the tin. There should be a good smearing of fat in the tin from the sausages. Whilst the tin is hot, crack in the eggs and immediately return the pan to the floor of the roasting oven. Cook for 2-3 minutes, and, depending on taste, turn the egg over and cook for 1-2 minutes. Serve on warm plates immediately.

Washing-up tip: Put the roasting pan to soak in hot soapy water straight away, otherwise the bits of egg can be difficult to clean off.

## AGA TOAST

This is a mystery to those who have not used an Aga before and cannot see the grill! The special Aga toaster – like a tennis racket – is needed. Most commercially baked bread is very moist, so to prevent sticking put the toaster under the lid of the boiling plate for about 1 minute to heat up. Remove and place in the bread to toast. Return to the boiling plate. If you like softer toast or are in a hurry, put the lid down, if not keep the lid up. Watch the toast, the time of toasting will vary with the thickness and type of bread and the temperature of your plate. Turn the toast over and do the second side.

## PORRIDGE

We love porridge in the winter and it is a great favourite with a variety of toppings. I have to say that lashings of soft brown sugar comes top of the list, though I like fruit or salt – my husband favours yoghurt. This is the easiest breakfast dish to prepare, though if you are an infrequent maker of porridge you may need to leave a reminder on the breakfast table that some is in the oven. I have given a recipe for 4, but I do know some people who make individual portions in a small cereal bowl with a saucer on top as a lid.

*1 cup rolled porridge oats*
*1 cup water*
*1 cup milk*
*pinch salt*

Put all the ingredients into a small saucepan, cover with a lid, put in the simmering oven for 8-12 hours. Stir and serve with milk or cream and your favourite flavouring.

## YOGHURT

Homemade yoghurt is very easy with the Aga supplying a constant, even temperature. If you and your family eat a lot of yoghurt it is certainly worth making. Of course you can add a variety of flavourings when it is made: fruits, jams, honey, nuts, or simply use plain in savoury dishes or as a substitute for cream. Do not be tempted to use your own homemade yoghurt as a starter for a new batch, it is always safer to start with a small pot of commercial yoghurt. You can use either ordinary yoghurt or Greek style – they use different cultures so will give you a different flavour.

*1 pint/575ml carton long-life milk – whole or skimmed*
*1 tbsp plain yoghurt*
*1 tbsp dried milk powder – to thicken*

Use very clean utensils. Mix the yoghurt and milk powder together in a bowl. Warm the milk – I stand mine in a jug on top of the Aga. Do not overheat the milk, this will kill the yoghurt bacteria. The milk should be warm to the touch. Blend the yoghurt mixture and the warm milk together.

Put a folded tea-towel or trivet on the simmering plate lid. Stand on a colander. Put the bowl containing the yoghurt mixture in the colander. Cover with a plate and leave 12 hours or overnight. The yoghurt should be set, thick and creamy. Store in the fridge.

# CAKES

During my Aga demonstrations I have heard so many people say, "I am told you cannot make a cake in an Aga." Nothing could be further from the truth, it is just a matter of knowing HOW to make a cake in an Aga.

The 4-oven Aga has a special baking oven, so cake-making is easy. Just use that oven for all cakes, except if you wish to cook a rich fruit cake overnight in the simmering oven. The 2-oven Aga has a very hot roasting oven, which may seem too hot for cooking at lower temperatures.

Each Aga should have a large plain baking sheet, made of aluminium, and known as the cold plain shelf. Cold is the most important word here. Store this shelf, not in the oven, but in a cool cupboard. The cold shelf is put in above cakes or biscuits to reduce the top heat, and to allow the cake to cook through

without burning. Always allow rising space and air circulation space – usually 2 runners above the oven shelf. If you are doing a large baking session, take the plain shelf out periodically to allow it to cool down and therefore become effective again. The cold plain shelf can be used as an oven shelf, and food such as scones can, of course, be put above it when it is being used as a cold shelf.

The other option for making deeper cakes that take several hours to bake is the Aga cake baker. The empty cake baker is heated up in the roasting oven while the cake is being made. The mixture is put into one of the tins provided, this is then put in the trivet and the whole thing put into the hot, empty cake baker. This is then returned to the roasting oven and the cake cooked for the required time. The cake baker insulates the cake, allowing it to cook through without burning. If converting a recipe check the cake during cooking as the final baking time may be shorter.

# BREAD AND YEAST COOKERY

Bread and yeast based dishes are so easy and successful using the Aga, not just because the roasting oven is so good for baking bread, but because the steady heat is perfect for warming and rising the bread dough. For a quick bread mix and for a store-cupboard standby the easy blend yeast in measured sachets is easy to use and quick. However, if you have time, try using fresh yeast and let the dough rise twice for a fuller flavour and better texture. Fresh yeast can be bought from health shops, bakers and the fresh-bake counters in supermarkets. Store in a plastic box in the fridge for about 10 days – should it go runny or smell rancid throw away and start with new yeast.

The choice of flour is largely personal. Organic flour comes in brown and white for bread making, or standard strong white or brown can be used, or a mixture of both. Special flours such as rye or granary may need to be bought at more specialist food shops. The quantities of liquids given in the recipes can only be guidelines because all flours vary in the amount of liquid they absorb. Try to make the dough as moist as possible, without being too sticky to handle, this will give a better finished product.

The main problem with breadmaking is trying not to kill the yeast. I warm the liquid by standing it on top of the Aga, that way it will be at blood heat and no hotter – it should be warm to the touch only. If the liquid is too hot the yeast will be killed before it can do its work! I have given a few basic recipes, but once you have mastered the art of breadmaking you can enjoy trying out new ideas and new recipes from other books.

# PRESERVES

Home-made jams and chutneys are easy to make, though a little time consuming. Quite a lot of the cooking can be done in the simmering oven, which removes the need to watch the preserving pan all the time and prevents burning on the bottom of the pan. Jams and chutneys make wonderful presents, particularly when presented with an attractive label or in a pretty jar.

I am giving an outline for basic methods of preservation, for more detail HMSO publish *Home Preservation of Fruit and Vegetables* which is a really good reference book. Alternatively, my few recipes will give you the basic method and other recipes can be used. A good, large preserving pan will be needed. I use a large deep catering pan with a lid. With mine, I can get the jam boiling well without too much spitting. The lid is useful when cooking slowly in the simmering oven. Collect jam jars with good, clean lids. I put mine through the dishwasher and keep them ready with their lids on. They only need warming in the simmering oven when needed. Labels and wax discs are needed.

When making jam or marmalade here are a few basic tips: Some fruit that needs slightly longer cooking, for instance, apricots, can be cooked in the simmering oven until softened. Choose a granulated or preserving sugar and always make sure it is dissolved before bringing to the boil, to prevent it crystallising

To test for a set, remove the boiling jam from the heat after 10-15 minutes rapid boil. Put about 1 teaspoon of jam on a cold plate. Chill the sample for 1-2 minutes. If the surface wrinkles when pushed with the finger, the setting point has been reached. If the setting point has not been reached boil again for 2-3 minutes and re-test. Too much boiling will give a syrupy jam. Cool the jam in the pan for a few minutes to prevent fruit rising to the top of the jar. Put the wax discs and lids on when the jam is either first put in the jar or when cold. Clean and label the jars when cold. Store in a cool, dark place.

Chutney is easily made in the Aga. The long, slow cooking which gives chutney its characteristic texture is done in the simmering oven. Again, a good-sized preserving pan is useful, and as the chutney is not boiled rapidly the pan can be about ²/₃ full. Jar lids need to be coated to prevent corrosion by the vinegar. Warm in the simmering oven before filling. Brown and white sugar can be used. Dark brown sugar will give a darker chutney and a rich flavour. Similarly, dark malt vinegar will colour the chutney, while for a lighter pickle you can use white wine vinegar.

# BOTTLING FRUIT

Bottling fruit has become fashionable again. It is much easier to use a jar of fruit for a quick pudding than thaw out fruit from the freezer. Do not be tempted to bottle vegetables, as the temperature in the Aga is not hot enough to make this safe. Use a Kilner jar for bottling – replacing the rubber rings or metal tops after each use. Check that the jar is in good condition – don't use any with chips. Wash and rinse the jars well. Choose fruit that is ripe, but not mushy or over-soft and bruised. For large fruits such as peaches, try to choose fruits of a similar size.

Bottling is done in the simmering oven and is very simple if the following method is used.

**1.** Line the large roasting tin with a few sheets of newspaper.

**2.** Stand the the clean jars in the tin – side by side but not touching.

**3.** Place tin and jars in the simmering oven for a few minutes to warm.

**4.** Prepare a syrup, about 8 oz/225g sugar to 1 pint/600ml water; the strength depends upon personal taste.

**5.** Remove the roasting tin from the oven and pack the jars with the prepared and washed fruits.

**6.** Pour in the boiling syrup, tapping each jar to bring air bubbles to the surface. Fill to within 1 inch/2.5cm of the top.

**7.** Fit on the lids – DO NOT SCREW ON ANY BANDS – this may cause the jar to explode.

**8.** Slide the roasting tin on the bottom set of runners of the simmering oven and heat for the following length of time.

| | |
|---|---|
| 1-2 jars | 1 hour |
| 3-6 jars | 2-3 hours |
| 7-10 jars | $2\frac{1}{2}$ – 4 hours |

The jars at the back will cook faster than the front. Look for tiny air bubbles; the fruit rising to the surface will indicate that the fruit is cooked. Light fruits may discolour if more than 6 bottles are done at a time; this is due to lower cooking temperatures. Remove from the oven, check that the rings and lids are in place – screw down firmly. Cool completely before checking to see if they are sealed – remove the screw band and lift the jar with the lid. If it remains secure, wipe and rescrew the band. Store in a dark place.

# CHRISTMAS

So many people seem to have their Aga fitted or "inherit" an Aga just before Christmas. My Aga workshop days in November and December and demonstrations at the Aga shop before Christmas are always over-subscribed.

A lot of people worry about the size of the oven or turkey, losing heat, getting everything done in time. Personally, I like to enjoy a relaxed Christmas Day, so I prepare as much as possible the day before. All the exact details for cooking will be found with each recipe. Give the temperature a little boost the night before to give extra capacity. A large turkey can be cooked slowly overnight, though of course the cooking method and time will have to be calculated according to the size of the turkey, your final planned eating time and what time you go to bed on Christmas Eve. A smaller 12 lb turkey will fit into the small roasting tin, giving room for another tin for the roast vegetables.

• When the turkey is out of the oven and resting in a warm spot for 15 minutes before carving, that is the time to crisp any roast vegetables – either at the very top of the roasting oven or directly on the floor.
• The Christmas pudding can be put on to steam for half an hour on the simmering plate early in the day, then transferred to the simmering oven where it will sit happily until needed.
• If the vegetables are ready and you are not, put on a knob of butter and put into the serving dishes and into the simmering oven to keep warm. All this should leave ample heat to quickly boil or steam green vegetables and to make the gravy.
• Sauces like breadsauce can be made early or the day before and warmed through in the simmering oven. With the quantity of food being cooked there is rarely space to warm plates and dishes. This is where I find a hot tray useful, or even a large washing-up bowl full of really hot water to put dishes and plates in.
• As a last resort, if cooking is taking a little longer than planned, have some nibbles handy.

If this is your first Christmas with an Aga, keep everything as simple as possible. Starters can be cold and prepared in advance. A second pudding could also be cold. Whatever, RELAX.

# SOUPS AND STARTERS

# ROAST NUTS
# FOR NIBBLES

I find assorted nuts done this way are really more-ish with drinks. If you like spicy nuts, stir in 1 teaspoon of garam masala with the salt. A jar of these makes an attractive present. It is also a good way to use up bits of left-over nuts, especially after Christmas.

*Take an assortment of nuts like pecans, brazils, walnuts, cashews, whole almonds and some sea salt*

Lay the nuts on a baking tray. Place on the oven shelf, about mid-way, in the roasting oven. Roast until slightly browning. Watch them because they burn quickly! Remove from the oven and immediately toss in some sea salt. The nuts should be slightly oily so that the salt will stick. If they seem dry, toss in 1 teaspoon of olive oil with the salt. Serve warm or cold. If putting in a jar, allow the nuts to cool completely before putting the lid on.

# GOUGERE
# CHEESE CHOUX PUFFS

I often make these as a hand-around starter for a supper party. They are best straight from the oven, but can also be eaten cold. The roasting oven needs to be up to temperature for their baking, so if the oven needs to be full, bake them in advance and warm them through before serving.

*3 oz/75g plain white flour*
*¼ tsp salt*
*shake of pepper*
*2 oz/50g butter – cut into cubes*
*2 eggs – beaten*
*3 oz/75g grated Gruyère*

Sieve flour, salt and pepper onto a sheet of greaseproof paper.

Put the butter into a saucepan with ¼ pint/150ml water. Stand the pan on the simmering plate and allow the butter to melt. Bring to the boil. Tip in the flour and beat well with a wooden spoon until the mixture leaves the sides of the pan clean. Cool.

Beat in the eggs – I use an electric mixer – until the mixture is smooth and glossy. Add the grated cheese and beat well.

Grease a baking tray. Spoon out about 12 dessertspoons of mixture. Bake on the third set of runners from the top in the roasting oven for 15-20 minutes. Check that the puffs are not browning too much – if they are, move the oven shelf to the floor of the oven. If not too brown, leave them nearer the top. Bake for a further 10 minutes. Serve warm or cold.

**Makes about 12.**

# CROUSTADES

......................................................

These easy to make nibbles are perfect for pre-dinner drinks or as a stand-up starter. Prepare ahead and bake as needed.

*15 slices white bread – from a sliced loaf*
*4 oz/100g butter*
*4 oz/100g blue cheese – Stilton or Roquefort*

TO FINISH:
*2 oz/50g melted butter*
*2 tsp caraway seeds*

Cut the crusts from the bread. Roll each slice with a rolling pin to flatten.
Cream the butter and the crumbled cheese together and spread this mixture over the bread slices. Roll up each slice tightly. Cut each roll in half.

Grease the small roasting tin. Pack in the bread rolls tightly, about 6 rolls wide by 5 rolls deep, with the ends of the slices underneath.

Brush the rolls with the melted butter. Sprinkle on the caraway seeds.

Hang the roasting tin on the top runners of the roasting oven for about 15 minutes until golden brown. Serve warm.

**Makes 15.**
......................................................

# P A T E   M A I S O N

...............................................

Pâtés are quick and easy to make, especially if you have a food processor or an electric mincer. They taste much nicer than commercial varieties and are much more economical. This is a coarse pâté, good for picnics and cold lunches with tasty bread or toast.

*2 lb/900g streaky pork rashers*
*¹/₂ lb/225g pig's liver*
*4 oz/100g streaky bacon*
*1 lb/450g minced lamb or veal*
*2 tbsp brandy*
*4 tbsp white wine*
*2 cloves garlic – peeled*
*ground black pepper*
*4 juniper berries – crushed*
*1 tsp salt*

Coarsely mince the pork rashers, liver and bacon. Combine in a mixing bowl all the ingredients and stir well to mix.

Put the mixture into a 2-pint capacity terrine or loaf tin.

For the 2-oven Aga, stand the oven shelf on the floor of the roasting oven, slide in the pâté tin and put the cold shelf one runner above the top of the tin. For the 4-oven Aga, put the oven shelf on the third set of runners from the top of the baking oven and then put in the pâté. Cook for about 2 hours, or until the pâté is shrinking from the sides of the tin. Cool and chill before slicing.

# CHICKEN TERRINE

..................................................

Chicken makes a lighter pâté, both in colour and flavour. A chicken terrine is good to serve with a good crisp salad and a variety of breads for lunch, or for a cold buffet table.

*2 lb/900g boneless chicken thighs*
*1 small onion – peeled*
*1 lb/450g sausage meat*
*1 tsp salt*
*pepper*
*1 tbsp finely chopped parsley*
*1 egg*
*8 rashers unsmoked streaky bacon*

Either mince or process the chicken and onion. Combine in a mixing bowl with the sausage meat, salt, pepper, parsley and egg. Mix thoroughly. Stretch out the rashers of bacon with the back of a knife blade. Use 4 rashers to line a 2½ pint/1 litre capacity terrine or loaf tin. Spoon in the pâté mixture, tap the tin on the work surface to remove any air bubbles. Lay on the remaining bacon rashers. Cover tightly with foil.

For the 2-oven Aga stand the oven shelf on the floor of the roasting oven, slide in the pâté tin and put the cold shelf one runner above the top of the tin. For the 4-oven Aga, put the oven shelf on the third set of runners from the top of the baking oven and then put in the pate. Cook for about 2 hours, or until the pâté is shrinking from the side of the tin. Cool and chill before slicing.

# HERB PATE

......................................................

This is an economical pâté to make for informal lunches or picnics. It is also popular in packed school lunches.

*1 lb/450g pig's liver*
*12 oz/350g streaky bacon*
*1 small onion – chopped*
*pinch of black pepper*
*³/₄ level tsp ground coriander*
*pinch grated nutmeg*
*¹/₄ tsp dried mixed herbs or 2 tbsp fresh chopped herbs*
*1 egg, beaten*

Wash the liver and trim off the bacon rind. Fry the bacon rind in a pan on the simmering plate until the fat runs, then discard the rind. Fry the onion in the fat until transparent.

Mince the liver and bacon 3 times, or process until fairly fine. Mix in the onion, pepper, coriander, nutmeg and herbs. Add the egg and mix well.

Grease and line a 2lb/1kg loaf tin. Spoon the mixture in and cover with foil. Stand the loaf tin in the small roasting tin. Pour round hot water to come half-way up the tin. Hang the roasting tin from the bottom runner of the roasting oven and cook for 1¹/₂ hours.

Remove from oven and weigh down the top with weights or baked bean tins until cold.

# VEGETABLE TERRINE

.......................................................

Attractively striped in cream and orange layers, this striking vegetable terrine is so easy to make and yet looks stunning when sliced. Serve it with a vinaigrette dressing which has 2 teaspoons of tomato purée added.

*1 large cauliflower – cut into florets and washed*
*1¹/₂ lb/675g carrots – peeled and sliced*
*salt and pepper*
*¹/₂ pint/300ml double cream*
*2 eggs*
*¹/₄ tsp freshly grated nutmeg*
*¹/₄ tsp ground coriander*

In separate saucepans cook the cauliflower and carrots in boiling, salted water. Cook the cauliflower until just tender and the carrots until well cooked. Drain well.

Purée the cauliflower in a blender or processor until smooth, then transfer the purée to a bowl. Purée the carrot in the same way and put in a separate bowl. Add 1 egg and half the cream to each bowl and beat in well. Season with salt and pepper. Stir the grated nutmeg into the cauliflower mixture and the coriander into the carrot mixture.

Grease a 2¹/₂ pint loaf tin or terrine tin. Put half the cauliflower in the base of the tin, and level it. Gently cover with a layer of half the carrot purée, followed by the remaining cauliflower and then the remaining carrot mixture. Tap the tin on the work surface to remove any air bubbles.

Cover the tin tightly with foil. For the 2-oven Aga put the oven shelf on the floor of the roasting oven. Put in the terrine, slide the cold shelf on the runner above the top of the tin. For the 4-oven Aga put the oven shelf on the third set of runners from the top of the baking oven. Put in the terrine. Bake for 1 hour or until firm.

Remove the terrine from the oven and allow it to cool slightly before turning out on to a serving plate. Slice with a sharp knife and serve with a little tomato flavoured vinaigrette. Serve hot or cold.

**Serves 8-10.**

..........

# CREAMY MUSHROOMS

Commercially grown button mushrooms often do not have much flavour. This recipe adds gentle flavouring. Serve the mushrooms on a bed of lettuce and chicory with maybe some bread to mop up any juices.

*1 oz/25g butter*
*1 lb/450g button mushrooms – wiped clean*
*1 tbsp flour*
*¹/₄ pint/150ml fresh milk*
*2 tbsp wholegrain mustard*
*2 tbsp fresh tarragon – chopped, or ¹/₂ tsp dried tarragon*
*3 tbsp soured cream*

Melt the butter in a large saucepan or frying pan on the simmering plate. Add the mushrooms and cook for 2 minutes. Stir in the flour and then the milk. Heat, stirring continuously, until the sauce thickens and is smooth. Simmer for 1-2 minutes.

Stir in the mustard, tarragon and soured cream. Serve hot on a bed of chicory and lettuce.

**Serves 4.**

# ASPARAGUS SOUP

The thicker stemmed asparagus can be used for this soup as it has more flavour. Serve chilled on a warm summer evening or gently warmed if the weather is cooler.

*1½ lb/675g asparagus*
*salt and pepper*
*2 small onions – peeled and chopped*
*1 oz/25g butter*
*2½ pints/1½ litres chicken stock*
*¼ pint/150ml single cream*

Cut the tips off the asparagus and simmer them gently in boiling, salted water until tender. Drain and refresh in cold water. Drain and reserve.

Trim the stalks of the asparagus and cut into 2 inch lengths. Melt the butter in a large saucepan on the simmering plate, add the asparagus stalks and the chopped onion. Stir, cover and cook for 5-10 minutes until soft but not browning. Add the stock and seasoning. Bring to the boil, cover and transfer to the simmering oven for about 45 minutes or until the asparagus is cooked.

Pass the soup through a blender or processor and then through a sieve to remove any woody stalk. Stir in the cream. Chill or warm through gently.

Serve garnished with the reserved asparagus tips.

**Serves 6-8.**

# COCK-A-LEEKIE SOUP

Cock-a-Leekie is a traditional Scottish soup that is more of a meal in a dish than a starter. A little beef can also be added for a more robust flavour.

*¹/₂ oz/15g butter*
*2 chicken quarters*
*12 oz/350g leeks, trimmed*
*2 pints/1 litre chicken stock*
*1 bouquet garni*
*salt and pepper*
*6 ready-to-eat prunes, halved and stoned*

Melt the butter in a large oven-proof saucepan and fry the chicken until golden brown.

Chop off the white part of the leek and dice it. Reserve the green part. Wash all the leeks well. Add the white part to the pan and cook for about 5 minutes until soft.

Add the stock, bouquet garni and seasoning to taste. Bring to the boil, cover and place in the simmering oven for 1 hour or until the chicken is tender.

Shred the green parts of the leek, add to the pan with the prunes and continue cooking for a further half hour.

To serve, remove the chicken, cut the meat into large pieces and discard the skin and bone. Put the meat into warmed soup bowls and pour over the soup. Serve hot.

**Serves 4 as a meal.**

# PARSNIP SOUP

......................................................

This is a thick, winter-warming soup. Serve with home-made bread for lunch or as a supper dish.

*1 oz/25g butter*
*1 large onion – peeled and chopped*
*1 level tsp curry powder (medium strength)*
*1 lb/450g parsnips – peeled and diced*
*¹/₂ lb/225g potatoes – peeled and diced*
*2 pints/1 litre chicken or vegetable stock*
*salt and pepper*
*single cream for serving*

Melt the butter in a large saucepan. Toss the onion in the butter and cook over a gentle heat until soft. Stir in the curry powder and cook for 1-2 minutes.

Add the diced parsnips and potatoes, Stirring well, then add the stock. Bring to the boil.

Cover and transfer to the simmering oven for about 1 hour, or until parsnips are soft.

Remove from the oven and pass through a food processor or liquidiser.

Season to taste. Heat through and serve with whirls of cream.

**Serves 6.**
......................................................

# TOMATO AND SWEET PEPPER SOUP

......................................................

I do not usually like tomato soup, but the addition of the red peppers makes it rich and sweet. This is a good winter soup using tinned tomatoes.

*2 oz/50g butter*
*12 oz/350g onion – chopped*
*2 large red peppers – deseeded and sliced*
*2 tbsp tomato purée*
*1 14oz/400g can tomatoes*
*2 tbsp chopped parsley*
*1 tsp sugar*
*1 bayleaf*
*¹/₄ tsp dried basil*
*¹/₄ tsp dried thyme*
*2 ¹/₂ pints/1¹/₂ litres light stock, chicken or vegetable*
*salt and pepper*

Melt the butter in a large saucepan on the simmering plate. Gently fry the onion and pepper until soft.

Stir in the remaining ingredients and bring to the boil. Transfer the pan to the simmering oven for 30-45 minutes.

Purée the soup in a blender or processor. Warm through and adjust the seasoning.

......................................................
**Serves 8 – 10.**
......................................................

# CELERY SOUP

This is one of my favourite all-year-round soups.

*1 celery head – cleaned and sliced*
*1 onion – chopped*
*1 oz/25g butter*
*1 oz/25g flour*
*³/₄ pint/450ml chicken or vegetable stock*
*1 blade mace*
*salt and pepper*
*¹/₂ pint/300ml milk*
*cream for serving*

Melt the butter in a pan on the simmering plate, stir in the chopped celery and onion, and cook until it is soft but not coloured.

Add the flour and stir well, cooking gently for 1 minute. Gradually add the stock, mace and a little salt and pepper.

Bring to the boil, cover and place in the simmering oven for 30 minutes.

Remove the pan from the oven and blend the soup. Rinse the pan, return the soup to the pan and add the milk. Heat through until piping hot. Taste and season.

Serve in warm bowls with a swirl of cream.

**Makes enough for 6 small or 4 large portions.**

# MAIN COURSES

# FISH

## FISH CAKES

Fish cakes made at home can be full of flavour and appeal to all the family. Ring the changes with different fish and herbs. Salmon and dill can be used to make something special. The herbs also give an attractive appearance.

*10 oz/275g haddock, skinned and boned*
*1 tbsp lemon juice*
*1 tbsp Worcestershire sauce*
*1 tbsp creamed horseradish*
*4 fl oz/100ml milk*
*1 tbsp fresh chives, snipped*
*1 tbsp fresh parsley, chopped*
*12 oz/350g maincrop potatoes, cooked and mashed*
*2 oz/50g fresh breadcrumbs*

Place the fish and milk in the small roasting tin, cover with foil and poach on the middle set of runners in the roasting oven for 10-15 minutes, until the fish is just flaking.

Remove from the oven, put the fish in a bowl, and flake fairly finely. Add the mashed potatoes, parsley, chives, horseradish, Worcestershire sauce and lemon juice. Mix all together, adding the poaching milk as needed to bind the fish cakes together. Shape into 4 fish cakes and coat with breadcrumbs. Clean the tin. If time allows, cover and chill for half an hour.

Smear a little cooking oil in the small roasting tin. Put to heat on the floor of the roasting oven. When the oil is hazing, put in the fish cakes and return the tin to the floor of the oven. Cook for 5 minutes, turn over and cook for a further 5 minutes until golden brown and sizzling hot. Serve immediately.

**Serves 4.**

# BAKED MACKEREL WITH GOOSEBERRY SAUCE

A lovely summer dish that can be eaten all year round if you put some gooseberries in the freezer for the winter. The tang of the gooseberries goes well with this oily fish – often a good buy at the fishmonger's. For a smooth sauce remove the pips by sieving.

*¹/₂ oz/15g butter*
*8 oz/225g gooseberries, topped and tailed*
*4 mackerel, cleaned, with heads removed*
*salt and pepper*
*lemon juice to taste*
*1 egg, beaten*

Melt the butter in a saucepan on the simmering plate, stir in the gooseberries and cover with a tightly fitting lid. Heat through for a couple of minutes and transfer to the simmering oven. Cook for about 20-30 minutes until tender.

Season the mackerel inside and out with salt, pepper and lemon juice. Make two or three diagonal slashes in the skin on each side of the fish. Place on the rack inside the roasting tin. Slide the tin onto the second set of runners from the top of the roasting oven and grill for 15-20 minutes, turning it half-way through, until tender.

Purée the gooseberries in a processor or sieve. Pour the purée into a clean pan, beat in the egg and heat gently, stirring. Season to taste.

Place the mackerel on warmed serving plates and spoon the sauce alongside.

**Serves 4.**

# FISHY PASTA

....................................................

This fish sauce is served with tagliatelle, but it can also be used as a base for a fish pie. Top with finely sliced, par-boiled potatoes or mashed potatoes and bake in the roasting oven for 20-30 minutes until piping hot and golden brown.

*1 lb/450g haddock or cod fillets*
*8 oz/225g smoked haddock or smoked cod fillets*
*2 oz/50g butter*
*6 oz/175g mushrooms – diced*
*1¹/₂ oz/35g flour*
*¹/₂ pint/300ml milk*
*¹/₄ pint/150ml water*
*6 spring onions – sliced*
*2 tbsp fresh parsley – chopped*
*4 oz/100g peeled prawns – thawed if frozen*
*salt and pepper*
*1¹/₄ lb/550g tagliatelle verde*

Place the fish in a roasting tin with the milk and water. Cover lightly with foil, hang the tin on the third set of runners from the top of the roasting oven and poach for 15-20 minutes until cooked. Heat water for pasta and cook according to instructions.

Melt the butter in a saucepan and fry the mushrooms until cooked. Remove them to a plate with a slotted spoon and keep warm in the simmering oven. Stir in the flour, cook for 1 minute and then gradually beat in the fish cooking liquor. Stir and boil the sauce, then add the mushrooms, spring onions, parsley and seasoning. Simmer gently for 5 minutes.

Meanwhile remove the skin and bones from the fish and then flake the flesh into largish pieces. Gently fold the fish and prawns into the sauce. Cover and keep warm in the simmering oven while the pasta is cooking.

Drain the pasta and top with the fish sauce.

**Serves 4-6.**
....................................................

# SALMON FILO TART

The filling in this rises like a soufflé and looks stunning. Serve with new potatoes and baby vegetables.

*4 oz/100g butter*
*4 oz/100g filo pastry*
*8 oz/225g salmon*
*1/2 pint/300ml milk*
*1 bay leaf*
*1 1/2 oz/35g plain flour*
*4 eggs – separated*
*2 tbsp chopped fresh dill*
*1 tbsp chopped chives*
*3 oz/75g grated Gruyère*
*salt and pepper*

Melt half the butter and brush the base and sides of 9-10 inch/23-25cm flan dish with it. Lay the pastry out on the worktop and brush the top sheet with melted butter. Lay a sheet of buttered pastry over the base of the flan dish. Continue in this way until the dish is lined. Cover with cling film. Chill.

Put the salmon in a small roasting tin. Pour on the milk, add the bay leaf. Put the tin in the centre of the roasting oven and cook the salmon for 15-20 minutes. Drain, reserving the milk.

Skin the salmon, remove the bones and flake the flesh.

Melt the remaining butter in a saucepan. Add the flour and the reserved milk, stirring well. Bring to the boil, and simmer until thick and smooth. Off the heat, beat in the egg yolks, herbs, cheese and seasoning.

Whisk the egg whites until softly stiff. Fold them into sauce, along with the salmon. Take the cling film off the pastry case and fill it with the sauce.

Place the flan dish on the floor of the roasting oven and bake for 25-30 minutes, until the filling is risen and golden. Serve warm.

**Serves 6.**

# PLAICE BAKED WITH CHEESE

..................................................

Use a finely grated mature cheese such as Sbrinz or Parmesan, for the best taste and appearance. The plaice can easily be replaced with lemon or Dover sole; whichever is used it needs to be in thin fillets.

*4 large fillets of plaice*
*¹/₂ oz/15g butter*
*3 tbsp dry white wine*
*juice of ¹/₂ a lemon*
*3 oz/75g grated Sbrinz or Parmesan cheese*
*black pepper*

Butter a large, shallow oven-proof dish. Wash and pat dry the fish. Season it on both sides with the pepper and lay it out in the dish.

Pour the wine and lemon juice round the fish and sprinkle with the finely grated cheese.

Have the oven shelf on the floor of the roasting oven, slide in the dish of fish and bake for 15-20 minutes until the fish is cooked and a light golden brown.

**Serves 4.**

..................................................

# KEDGEREE

........................................................

This is a traditional breakfast dish, but I like it for supper. The quantities can be increased easily for a crowd, and can be assembled at the last minute. Good for a brunch party.

*1 lb/450g smoked haddock fillets*
*1 lemon – sliced*
*pepper*
*3 eggs – hard-boiled and shelled*
*12 oz/350g cooked long-grain rice (about 5 oz/150g uncooked)*
*2 oz/50g butter – softened*
*2 tbsp parsley – chopped*
*3 fl oz/75ml single cream*

Place the fish in the small roasting tin and cover with water. Sprinkle with pepper and lay on half the lemon slices. Slide the tin into the roasting oven, on the third set of runners from the top and cook for 15-20 minutes, depending upon the size and shape of the fillets, until the fish is tender.

Drain the fish, remove and discard the skin and bones. Flake the flesh. Chop the eggs.

Rinse out the roasting tin, mix in it the rice, butter, fish, eggs, parsley and cream. Cover with foil, hang on the bottom set of runners of the roasting oven to heat through – about 10-15 minutes.

Stir and garnish with lemon slices and a little parsley.

**Serves 4-6.**
........................................................

# SAVOURY FISH CRUMBLE

Savoury crumbles are delicious for family meals. Ring the changes with different fish – cod, haddock, whiting. This can be prepared in advance and reheated in the roasting oven until hot right through and golden on the top.

*1-1½ lb/450-700g white fish*
*milk for poaching*
*1 tbsp oil*
*4 leeks – trimmed, washed and sliced*
*4 sticks celery – scrubbed and sliced*
*6 oz/150g button mushrooms – wiped and halved*
*4 hard-boiled eggs – peeled and quartered*
*¾ pint/450ml milk*
*1 oz/40g flour*
*1½ oz/40g butter*
*salt and pepper*

**CRUMBLE TOPPING**
*6 oz/150g wholemeal breadcrumbs*
*4 oz/100g cheese – grated*
*2 tbsp chopped fresh herbs or 2 tsp mixed dried herbs*
*1 oz/25g butter*

Poach the fish in the milk until cooked, about 10-15 minutes in the roasting oven. In a saucepan heat the oil and gently fry the leeks and celery. When softening, add the mushrooms and cook until soft. Remove any skin and bones from the fish. Put the fish mixture into a shallow ovenproof dish and add the eggs and vegetables. Make a white sauce with the milk, flour and butter. Season and pour over the fish. Mix the breadcrumbs, grated cheese and herbs together and sprinkle over. Dot with slivers of butter and bake, with the oven shelf on the floor of the roasting oven, for 30-40 minutes until golden brown.

Serves 4.

# MEAT, POULTRY AND GAME

## ITALIAN-STYLE STEAK

This steak will look more professional if it is cooked in the ridged cast-iron pan, but this is not essential. Cooking in the oven not only saves heat wastage but all smells disappear up the chimney.

*4 thinly cut rump steaks*
*2 cloves garlic – peeled and crushed*
*salt and pepper*
*1 lb/450g tomatoes – skinned and chopped*
*1 tbsp fresh basil – chopped*
*2 tbsp parsley – chopped*
*olive oil*

Heat the pan on the floor of the roasting oven until really hot, 5-8 minutes. When hot, place in the steaks and cook quickly for 2-3 minutes, browning both sides.

Add garlic, salt and pepper. Stir in the tomatoes and herbs and a little olive oil if necessary. Cook for 3-5 minutes until the tomatoes are softened but still holding their shape.

Serve immediately with new potatoes and green salad.

**Serves 4.**

# BEEF IN STOUT

........................................

This easy-to-prepare casserole has a rich, tasty gravy. The stewing steak benefits from long, slow cooking.

*2 lb/900g stewing steak – cubed*
*¹/₂ oz/15g butter*
*1 tbsp vegetable oil*
*4 medium onions – sliced*
*8 oz/225g button mushrooms – wiped and halved*
*salt and pepper*
*2 tbsp flour*
*¹/₂ pint/300ml stout*
*1 bay leaf*
*1 tsp soft brown sugar*

Heat the butter and oil in a large, flameproof casserole and brown the meat. Remove the meat to a plate.

Add the onions and cook until softening. Stir in the mushrooms, adding a little more oil if necessary. Stir in the flour and a seasoning of salt and pepper.

Return the meat to the casserole dish, pour in the stout, add the bay leaf and sugar. Stir well, cover and bring to a gentle boil. Boil for 2-3 minutes then transfer to the simmering oven for about 3 hours or until the meat is tender. Serve with creamy mashed potatoes and lightly cooked carrots.

**Serves 6.**
........................................

# CLASSIC BEEF CASSEROLE

The Aga is ideal for cooking casseroles slowly, as it develops rich flavours and tenderises the meat. This recipe has a strong French influence and can easily be adapted to suit whatever ingredients are to hand. Serve with crisp baked potatoes and very fresh green vegetables, or have a crispy salad to follow.

*2 lb/900g good braising steak or skirt, cut into large squares*
*6 oz/175g unsmoked streaky bacon, in one piece if possible, then diced*
*2 onions – peeled and sliced*
*2 carrots – peeled and sliced*
*2 tomatoes – skinned and sliced*
*2 cloves garlic – peeled*
*bouquet garni*
*2 tbsp olive oil*
*¼ pint/150ml red wine*

In the bottom of a flameproof casserole pour the olive oil, then place in the bacon and prepared vegetables. Lay the meat on top. Bury the garlic and the bouquet garni in the centre.

Stand the casserole, uncovered, on the floor of the roasting oven and start cooking.

After about 10-15 minutes put the wine in a small pan on the boiling plate. When it is boiling, set the wine alight and allow the alcohol to burn off. When the flames have died down pour the wine over the casserole. Cover with a lid and allow the casserole to come to the boil. Transfer to the simmering oven for 3 hours.

To serve, dish the meat, bacon and vegetables onto a warm serving platter. Skim off most of the fat from the liquid, and remove the bouquet garni. Heat the sauce to bubbling on the simmering plate and pour over the meat.

**Serves 6-8.**

# BASIC BOLOGNESE SAUCE

This is such a useful standby. Make a large batch and freeze in portions. I use this meat sauce with spaghetti and as a filling for lasagne. Cook gently in the simmering oven for a good flavour and tender meat. In our family we like a rich tomato sauce, so I use creamed tomatoes or passata, but canned tomatoes can be used.

*1 lb/450g lean minced beef*
*1 tbsp olive oil*
*1 onion – chopped*
*4 oz/100g sliced mushrooms*
*1 clove garlic – crushed*
*1 carton creamed tomatoes*
*¹/₄ pint/150ml red wine*
*1 bay leaf*
*¹/₂ tsp dried oregano or about 10 basil leaves, torn*

Heat the olive oil in a saucepan on the simmering plate, add the onion and cook until soft but not browned. Add the mushrooms and the garlic and cook until softening. Remove to a plate.

Move the pan to the boiling plate, add the meat, break up and brown, stirring. Return to the simmering plate, stir in the mushroom and onion mixture, tomatoes, red wine, bay leaf and herbs. Bring to the boil, stirring. Cover with a lid and transfer to the simmering oven for 1 hour.

Serve with cooked spaghetti and grated Swiss Sbrinz or use as a filling for lasagne.

**Serves 4.**

# LASAGNE

.................................................

This dish can be made in advance, which is useful as it can be fairly time-consuming to make. The recipe uses the usual meat sauce, but lasagne can also be made with fish or vegetables – pre-cook either and add to a creamy sauce before layering with the lasagne. Finish off with the sauce and cheese topping. Lasagnes are easier to make and serve in an oblong dish.

*Meat sauce using 1lb/450g meat – as for basic Bolognese sauce*
*9 oz/250g packet ready to use lasagne*
*³/₄ pint/450ml single cream*
*2 oz/50g plain flour*
*salt and pepper*
*3 oz/75g strongly flavoured, finely grated cheese e.g. Gruyère*

Mix the flour and the cream together. Season this sauce with salt and pepper.

Butter an oblong dish. Pour a thin layer of sauce in the bottom. Layer on the sheets of lasagne followed by a layer of meat sauce. Repeat, finishing with lasagne. Pour on any remaining sauce and sprinkle with grated cheese.

For the 2-oven Aga, put the shelf on the floor of the oven, put in the lasagne and bake for 45 minutes. If it is browning too rapidly, slide the cold shelf two runners above the dish. For the 4-oven Aga, put the oven shelf on the bottom set of runners of the baking oven. Put in the lasagne and bake for 45 minutes. If the oven is too hot and the top is browning too quickly, cover the top with a sheet of foil. If the lasagne is cooked through and you are not quite ready to serve it, keep it warm in the simmering oven.

Serves 4-6.
.................................................

# QUORMA LAMB CURRY

This is more a spicy dish than a hot curry. My family like spicy, tasty food but are not keen on hot curries, so this is perfect. The curry will sit happily in the simmering oven for a longer time if you are delayed.

*1 lb/450g trimmed, boned shoulder of lamb, cubed*
*¹/₂ tbsp grated fresh root ginger*
*salt*
*2 oz/50g butter*
*1 onion, sliced*
*2 cloves of garlic, chopped*
*1 tsp whole cardamom pods*
*1 tsp whole coriander seeds*
*1 tsp whole cloves*
*1 tsp black peppercorns*
*2 oz/50g creamed coconut, grated*
*2 oz/50g double cream*
*¹/₂ tsp ground turmeric*
*1 tsp sugar*
*1 fl oz/25ml lemon juice*

Mix the lamb, ginger and a little salt.

Melt the butter and sweat the onions and garlic slowly for 5 minutes.

Slit the cardamom pods and remove the black seeds. Grind to a powder with the coriander, cloves and peppercorns. Sprinkle over the onions and cook for 1 minute.

Add the meat and remaining ingredients to the pan. Mix well, cover and get piping hot on the simmering plate.

Transfer to the simmering oven for 1¹/₂ to 2 hours. Taste and adjust seasoning. Serve with rice.

**Serves 4.**

# LEMON AND LAMB MEATBALLS

The lemon imparts a fresh taste to lamb. The meatballs can be made in advance and then browned and cooked when needed.

*1 lb/450g minced lamb*
*1 onion – grated*
*1 potato – peeled and grated*
*1 egg – beaten*
*salt and pepper*
*1 tbsp chopped parsley*
*1 oz/25g flour*
*1 oz/25g butter*
*¼ pint/150ml light stock*
*finely grated rind and juice of 1 lemon*
*2 tsp cornflour blended with a little water*

Put the lamb, onion, potato, egg, salt and pepper and parsley in a bowl and mix well. Take tablespoons of the mixture and form into balls. Roll in flour and chill in the fridge for about half an hour.

Melt the butter in a flameproof casserole on the simmering plate. Fry the meatballs until browned. Pour in the stock, lemon juice and rind. Cover and bring to the boil. Transfer to the simmering oven and cook for about 1 hour.

Return the casserole to the simmering plate. Stir in the slaked cornflour, bring to the boil, stirring to thicken the sauce.

Taste, adjust seasoning and serve.

**Serves 4.**

# SWEET AND SOUR PORK

I love the flavours of sweet and sour pork, but I am not keen on deep-fat frying, so I make a casserole to cook the meat and add crispy vegetables towards the end of the cooking time. Serve with plain rice.

### MARINADE
*1 lb/450g lean pork – cut into cubes*
*1 tbsp dry sherry*
*1 tbsp light soy sauce*

### SAUCE
*¹/₄ pint/150ml chicken stock*
*1 tbsp oil*
*1 tbsp soy sauce*
*1¹/₂ tbsp cider or white wine vinegar*
*1 tbsp sugar*
*1 tbsp tomato purée*
*¹/₂ green pepper – finely sliced*
*¹/₂ red pepper – finely sliced*
*2 carrots – sliced*
*4 spring onions – chopped*
*1 small bag bean shoots*
*1 tsp cornflour, blended with a little water*

Toss the meat in the sherry and the 1 tablespoon soy sauce. Marinate for at least half an hour to tenderise the meat and add flavour. Heat the oil in a flameproof casserole and brown the meat. Stir in the chicken stock, soy sauce, vinegar, sugar, tomato purée and carrots. Bring to the boil, put in the bottom of the simmering oven for 45 minutes to 1 hour.

Return to the simmering plate, stir in the peppers and spring onions and simmer for 10 minutes. Stir in the cornflour paste and the bean shoots. Stir well until heated through. Taste and serve.

**Serves 4.**

# POT ROAST OF PORK WITH RED CABBAGE AND APPLE

..............................................

Use a rolled boneless pork joint for this recipe, it will be perfect for pot roasting. Red cabbage and apple go very well together and add moistness to the pork.

*3 tbsp red wine vinegar*
*1 small red cabbage – finely shredded*
*1 cooking apple – peeled, cored and sliced*
*1 tbsp demerara sugar*
*1 tbsp plain flour*
*salt and pepper*
*2 lb/900g boneless pork joint, rolled*

Bring a large pan of water to the boil. Add 1 tablespoon of the vinegar and the cabbage. Bring back to the boil then drain well.

Place the cabbage and apple slices in a casserole dish. Toss in the sugar, flour and remaining vinegar. Season to taste and stir well.

Sprinkle the joint with salt and pepper. Place on top of the cabbage and put the lid on.

Put the oven shelf on the floor of the roasting oven, or for a 4-oven Aga on the third set of runners from the top of the baking oven, and bake the pork for 2 hours, until the meat is tender. Serve the pork sliced, with the apple and cabbage, and some mashed potatoes.

**Serves 6-8.**
..............................................

# PORK CHOPS WITH CHEESE AND BEER

......................................................

These chops are grilled and have a delicious topping. The chops can also be served plain, cooked in the same way without the topping.

*4 pork loin chops*
*4 oz/100g good Cheddar cheese, grated*
*1 tsp mustard*
*3 tbsp brown ale*

Place the rack in the small roasting tin and lay on the chops. Slide the roasting tin onto the top set of runners of the roasting oven and grill the chops for 10-12 minutes, depending upon thickness. Turn them over and cook for a further 10-12 minutes until cooked through.

Mix together the cheese, mustard and ale and spread over the chops. Return to the grill until the cheese has melted.

Serve garnished with tomato and watercress.

**Serves 4.**
......................................................

# PORK AND PARSNIP CASSEROLE

A truly delicious casserole if you like the taste of fresh ginger. During the slow cooking the parsnips take on the ginger flavour which goes very well with the pork. Any cut of pork can be used provided it is not too fatty.

*1¹/₂ lb/675g pork, diced*
*1 lb/450g parsnips*
*8 oz/225g small onions*
*2 tbsp oil*
*1 clove garlic*
*³/₄ pint/450ml light stock*
*1 tbsp soy sauce*
*1 tbsp golden syrup*
*2 tbsp white wine vinegar*
*¹/₂ inch fresh root ginger – peeled and grated*
*1 level tbsp cornflour*
*salt and pepper*

Cut parsnips into 1-inch cubes. Peel and quarter the onions, keeping the roots intact. Peel the garlic.

Heat the oil in a frying pan with the garlic. Brown the meat and remove it to a casserole dish. Brown the parsnips and onions in the frying pan. Remove and discard the garlic. Stir in the stock, soy sauce, golden syrup, vinegar and grated ginger. Bring to the boil and pour over the meat. Cover the casserole.

Ensure the casserole is piping hot, then transfer to the simmering oven for 2 hours.

Mix the cornflour with a little water. Stir into the casserole and heat on the simmering plate or, if the casserole dish is not flameproof put it in the roasting oven, until the sauce has thickened. Adjust the seasoning and serve.

**Serves 4-6.**

# CHICKEN AND PRUNE CASSEROLE

This makes a rich chicken dish, easy to make. I find it a comforting dish for cold winter days.

*6-8 chicken portions*
*4 garlic cloves*
*2 level tsp dried mixed herbs*
*2 tbsp red wine vinegar*
*4 fl oz/100ml oil*
*8 oz/225g pitted, ready to eat prunes*
*salt and pepper*
*1/2 pint/300ml dry white wine*
*1 oz/25g demerara sugar*
*1 level tsp cornflour*
*1/4 pint/150ml chicken stock*

Place the chicken in a large, non-metallic bowl. Add the sliced garlic cloves, mixed herbs, wine vinegar, oil, prunes and seasoning and mix well. Cover and marinate in the fridge overnight.

Remove the chicken from the marinade and fry it until golden brown in a little oil skimmed from the marinade. Transfer to a flameproof casserole dish. Add the marinade mixture and the wine. Sprinkle in the sugar.

Bring to the boil on the simmering plate, boil for 2-3 minutes, cover and place in the roasting oven, the shelf on the floor of the oven, for 45 minutes.

Blend the cornflour and chicken stock. Remove the casserole from the oven. Serve the chicken onto a plate, keep warm in the simmering oven. Add the stock mixture to the marinade, heat it on the simmering plate, stirrring until thickened. Pour the sauce over the chicken.

Garnish with chopped parsley and serve.

**Serves 6-8.**

# HERB BAKED CHICKEN

I love to make this in the summer when there are plenty of fresh herbs to add flavour to plain chicken. I add a bunch of mixed fresh herbs to the bread in the food processor and everything is then chopped together. The amount of herbs used depends upon taste.

*4 chicken portions – skinless*
*1 egg*
*seasoned flour*
*6 oz/175g breadcrumbs*
*1 tbsp finely chopped parsley*
*2 tbsp finely chopped mixed herbs or 2 tsp dried mixed herbs*
*salt and pepper*
*grated rind of ¹/₂ a lemon*
*2 oz/50g butter*

Beat the egg in a shallow dish. Spoon a little seasoned flour onto a plate.

Measure the breadcrumbs into a basin, stir in the parsley, herbs, salt, pepper and lemon rind. Melt the butter in a basin on top of the Aga, and stir into the crumbs and fork well.

Roll the chicken portions first in the flour, then in the egg and finally in the breadcrumbs, patting them on firmly. Place the chicken in the small roasting tin, and slide it into the roasting oven on the third set of runners from the top. Bake for 30-40 minutes until crisp, golden and cooked through – there should be no pink juices when pierced with a sharp knife.

Serve with a good green salad and crusty bread.

**Serves 4.**

# CHICKEN IN RED WINE WITH RAISINS

The sauce for this casserole dish is rich and spicy and makes a lovely winter dish. During cooking the raisins and apricots become plump and juicy.

*1/2 pint/300ml red wine*
*3 tbsp red wine vinegar*
*2 oz/50g seedless raisins*
*4 oz/100g no-soak dried apricots – halved*
*1 tsp ground ginger*
*1 tsp ground cinnamon*
*1/2 inch/1cm piece fresh root ginger – peeled and grated*
*4 cloves*
*4 juniper berries – lightly crushed*
*4 chicken portions*
*2 tbsp flour*
*salt and pepper*
*knob of butter*
*1 tbsp vegetable oil*
*1/2 pint/300ml chicken stock*

Put the wine, vinegar, raisins, apricots, ground ginger, cinnamon, fresh ginger, cloves and juniper berries in a non-metallic dish. Add the chicken pieces and cover with the marinade. Cover and leave to marinate for at least 3-4 hours or overnight.

Remove the chicken from the marinade and pat dry on kitchen paper. Season the flour with salt and pepper then coat the chicken with the flour. Heat the oil and butter in a flameproof casserole dish, add the chicken, skin side down, and fry until golden brown. Turn and brown the other side. Lift the chicken out and put to one side. Pour off any excess fat. Pour the marinade and stock into the casserole dish, bring to the boil, stirring, return the chicken. Boil for 2-3 minutes and then transfer, covered, to the simmering oven for 1-1½ hours until the chicken is tender. Transfer the chicken to a warm plate, boil the liquid to reduce to a thicker sauce. Pour over the chicken. Lovely with boiled rice.

**Serves 4.**

# TURKEY BURGERS

..................................................

Home-made burgers are much nicer than anything bought in the shops. They are quick and easy to make, either by hand or in a processor. Turkey meat is low in fat and healthy, but it does need some flavouring. Cook these in the oven and serve with home-made oven chips (see page 82).

*1 small onion – finely chopped*
*1 lb/450g minced turkey*
*2 oz/50g fresh breadcrumbs or porridge oats*
*grated rind of ¹/₂ a small lemon*
*2 tbsp chopped parsley*
*8 streaky bacon rashers, rindless*
*salt and pepper*
*a little oil*

If making by hand, fry the onion in a little oil until soft, then combine with the minced turkey meat, breadcrumbs, lemon rind, parsley and salt and pepper to taste. Alternatively put the onion in the processor and chop it finely. Add all the ingredients except the bacon and process them together.

Shape into eight burgers. Cut each rasher in half lengthways, and wrap two rashers round each burger in a cross formation. Place the burgers on a baking tray and drizzle a little oil over them. Put the tray of burgers on the floor of the roasting oven for 15 minutes, then put the oven shelf on the top set of runners in the roasting oven and move the tray of burgers up for 10-15 minutes to give a crisp finish to the bacon.

Makes 8 burgers.
..................................................

# STIR-FRY

Many people think they cannot stir-fry on their Aga. I find it very successful using the boiling plate and a large frying pan. This recipe can be adapted for vegetarians and meat eaters alike. Tofu, a bean curd, has little flavour of its own, so it is a good idea to marinate before cooking. The same can be said of turkey or chicken strips, so treat them in the same way.

*2 tbsp soy sauce*
*2 tbsp dry sherry*
*2 tbsp orange juice*
*2 spring onions – sliced*
*1 clove garlic – crushed*
*8 oz/225g tofu- cubed or 12 oz/350g chicken or turkey in strips*
*2 tbsp sesame oil*
*1 oz/25g flaked almonds*
*1 red pepper – cored, de-seeded and sliced*
*6 oz/175g mange-tout peas, topped, tailed and halved*
*4 oz/100g button mushrooms – sliced*
*8 oz/225g beansprouts*
*2 tbsp sesame seeds, toasted (place on a baking tray in the top of the*
*roasting oven for 2-5 minutes – watch them as they burn easily)*

Mix the soy sauce, sherry, orange juice, onions and garlic in a basin. Toss in either the tofu or the meat strips. Cover and leave to marinate for 1 hour. Heat the oil in a large frying pan, add the almonds, fry for 1 minute to brown on all sides, remove with slotted spoon to a plate, and then keep warm in the simmering oven. Add the tofu cubes or meat strips to the hot pan and stir-fry until they begin to brown, 2-3 minutes for the tofu, 5 minutes for the meat. Remove them to the plate in the simmering oven.

Add the peppers and mange-tout peas, stir-fry for about 2 minutes, stir in the mushrooms and beansprouts, and cook for another minute. Add the almonds and the marinade and cook for 2 minutes. Stir in the tofu or meat, heat through and serve, sprinkled with the sesame seeds.

Serves 4.

# LIVER STROGANOFF

...................................................

This is a quick and easy dish, tasty enough to serve to guests and liked by those uncertain about eating liver. It is nothing like the well-cooked liver of school days! Hot ribbon noodles, such as tagliatelle, go well.

*½ oz/12g butter*
*1 medium onion – skinned and sliced*
*1 lb/450g lamb's liver – cut into strips*
*1 tbsp flour*
*4 oz/100g button mushrooms*
*¼ pint/150ml stock*
*4 tomatoes – skinned and roughly chopped*
*1 tbsp Worcestershire sauce*
*salt and pepper*
*5 fl oz soured cream or thick yoghurt*

Melt the butter in a large frying pan and gently fry the onion until soft and cooked.

Put the liver, salt and pepper and flour in a plastic bag. Shake to coat the liver in flour. Add the liver to the pan along with the mushrooms. Fry for 5 minutes, stirring well. Add the stock and bring to the boil.

Stir in the tomatoes and Worcestershire sauce. Simmer for 3-4 minutes. Stir in the cream and reheat without boiling. Serve.

**Serves 4.**

...................................................

# SAUSAGE PAPRIKA

.................................................

This is a wonderful way to cook sausages. Everything is cooked in one dish in the oven. Just serve with baked potatoes for a warming, economical dish.

*1 lb/450g herb sausages*
*1 tbsp oil*
*2 large onions – chopped*
*4 oz/100g mushrooms – sliced*
*15 oz/425g can chopped tomatoes*
*2 tbsp tomato purée*
*2 tsp paprika*
*salt*
*5 oz/150g carton plain yoghurt*
*chopped parsley to garnish*

Lay the sausages in a single layer in an oven-proof dish. Put the oven shelf on the second set of runners down in the roasting oven, put in the sausages and brown them for about 5-10 minutes.

Remove them from the dish to a plate in the simmering oven to keep warm. Pour oil into the oven-proof dish and put on the floor of the roasting oven, heat for 1-2 minutes. Stir in the onions and cook for 10 minutes, stirring occasionally. Add the mushrooms, stir and cook for 4-5 minutes. Stir in the tomatoes, purée, paprika and a pinch of salt. Return the sausages to the dish, and cover with a lid or foil. Put the shelf on the bottom set of runners, put in the sausage dish for 30-40 minutes.

Stir in the yoghurt, return to the oven to heat through. Sprinkle with chopped parsley.

Serve with baked potatoes.

**Serves 4.**

.................................................

# VENISON CASSEROLE

Venison is now readily available in supermarkets and makes a richly flavoured casserole. This is an ideal traditional Aga dish, cooked gently in the simmering oven to give tender meat and a delicious flavour.

*1¹/₂ lb/675g casserole venison – diced*
*2 onions – peeled and sliced*
*1 clove garlic – peeled and crushed*
*2 tbsp flour*
*2 tbsp oil*
*salt and pepper*
*¹/₄ pint/150ml stock*
*¹/₂ pint/300ml red wine*
*1 tbsp sage – chopped or 1 tsp dried sage*
*4 oz/100g button mushrooms*

Season the flour with the salt and pepper, then toss the diced meat in it.

Heat the oil in a flameproof casserole and cook the onions gently until softened. Stir in the meat and cook until browned. Stir in the garlic, stock, wine and sage. Bring to the boil, cover and transfer to the simmering oven for 2-3 hours until the meat is tender.

Stir in the mushrooms and return to the oven for a further 15-20 minutes. Serve with creamy, mashed potatoes.

**Serves 4-6.**

# ROAST DUCK WITH GREEN PEAS

..........................................

Duckling is less fatty now, but can still produce a lot of fat during the cooking process, so cooking this in the roasting tin with the grill rack makes for a moist but not fatty meat.

*1 oven-ready duckling, about 4¹/₂ lbs/2kg in weight*
*salt and pepper*
*16 (approx) small onions or shallots – skinned*
*2 oz/50g streaky bacon rashers – rindless and diced*
*1 lb/450g frozen peas*
*4 tbsp chicken stock or white wine*

Weigh the duckling, prick the skin all over and rub with salt. Stand it on the high setting of the rack in the small roasting tin and loosely cover it with foil. Roast on the bottom set of runners of the roasting oven for 30 minutes per 1 lb/450g.

Half an hour before the end of the cooking time, remove the duckling and rack, and drain off most of the fat from the roasting tin. Stand the roasting tin on the simmering plate and brown the onions in the hot fat. Add the bacon and stir for 2-3 minutes until the fat runs. Mix the peas into the onion mixture with some salt and pepper. Stir in the stock or wine. Return the duckling, on the rack, to the roasting tin and return to the oven, uncovered. Cook for a further 30 minutes.

Serve on a warm platter, surrounded by the vegetables.

**Serves 4.**
..........................................

# PIGEON AND PLUM CASSEROLE

Pigeons and plums are in season together and combine in this casserole to make a slightly sweet and sour mixture. The cooking time for the pigeons will depend on how young and tender they are.

*1 oz/25g butter*
*1 tbsp vegetable oil*
*4 pigeons – dressed*
*2 tsp flour*
*1 medium onion – skinned and chopped*
*2 cloves*
*1 bouquet garni*
*¹/₄ pint/150ml port*
*1 lb/450g plums – stoned and halved*
*salt and pepper*
*a little grated nutmeg*

Heat the butter and oil in a flameproof casserole. Coat the pigeons in the flour and then fry them until browned on all sides. Remove them to a warm plate.

Fry the onion in the casserole until softening, return the pigeons to the pan and add the bouquet garni, cloves and port. Arrange the plums over the top. Cover with a tightly fitting lid. Bring to the boil and then transfer to the simmering oven for about 2 hours, until the pigeons are tender.

Transfer the pigeons and plums to a serving plate. Boil the juices to thicken, season with salt, pepper and nutmeg and pour over the pigeon.

**Serves 4.**

# PIZZA

...............................................

I use a standard bread dough enriched with some olive oil for my pizzas. Some freshly chopped herbs, or a teaspoon of dried herbs can also be added. You can of course also use a packet of pizza base mix. A variety of toppings can be used, but a good tomato base is always needed. In winter I make a topping using canned tomatoes, but in summer, when tomatoes have more flavour and are more plentiful, I spread the base with chopped tomatoes and then put on my toppings.

### TOMATO SAUCE
*1 tbsp olive oil*
*1 onion, finely chopped*
*1 clove garlic, peeled and crushed*
*¹/₂ tsp dried basil*
*1 tbsp tomato purée*
*1 x 14 oz/400g can chopped tomatoes – drained*
*salt and pepper*

Heat the oil in a saucepan, stir in the chopped onion and the garlic and cook until softened.

Stir in the remaining ingredients, bring to the boil, cover and transfer to the simmering oven for half an hour.

Spread over the pizza bases, leaving ¹/₄ inch/5mm border all round. Finish with a selection of toppings.

### PIZZA BASE
*1 lb/450g bread flour*
*1 tsp salt*
*1 tsp herbs*
*1 sachet of easy-blend yeast*
*4 tbsp olive oil*
*¹/₂ pint/300ml warm water, approximately*

Measure the flour into a mixing bowl and stir in the salt and yeast. Stir in the olive oil and herbs. Blend in enough warm water to make a manageable dough

..............

for kneading.

Knead the dough on a floured worktop for at least 5 minutes until pliable. Divide the dough into 2 and roll to 10-inch rounds.

I like my pizzas to have a very crispy base so I brush the pizza with oil and turn it over onto a baking tray. If you prefer, you may just place them, slightly floury, on a baking tray.

Fold a tea-towel on top of the simmering plate lid and stand the pizza base tray on top to rise for about 30 minutes.

Meanwhile prepare the topping.

**Makes 2 large pizzas.**

### A FEW TOPPING SUGGESTIONS
*•Chopped black olives, red pepper slices and crumbled feta cheese.*
*•Just lashings of grated Gruyère.*
*•Salami slices, chopped black olives and Mozzarella cheese grated.*
*•Thinly sliced streaky bacon and finely sliced mushrooms.*
*•Slices of finely sliced ham and pineapple pieces.*

### BAKING THE PIZZA
When the base is risen and fluffy and the toppings are ready, slide the pizza tray onto the floor of the roasting oven for 15 minutes – this will ensure a crisp base. Have the oven shelf on the second set of runners from the top and after 15 minutes transfer the pizza to the shelf for a further 10-15 minutes to cook the topping.

# VEGETABLES AND VEGETARIAN

## WENSLEYDALE AND WATERCRESS TART

I make this in the small roasting tin, which is useful if you are catering for a crowd. The filling can be altered but the basic quantity of eggs and milk and cream are given.

*1 lb/450g shortcrust pastry*
*6 eggs*
*¹/₂ pint/300ml single cream*
*¹/₂ pint/300ml milk*
*salt and pepper*
*1 bunch watercress – washed and finely chopped*
*grating of fresh nutmeg*
*8 oz/225g Wensleydale – crumbled or grated*

Using the shortcrust pastry, line the small roasting tin. Beat together the eggs, cream, milk, salt and pepper. Stir in the chopped watercress and nutmeg. Add the cheese. Pour the mixture into the prepared pastry case. Put the roasting tin on the floor of the roasting oven and bake for 30-40 minutes until the filling is set.

### VARIATIONS:

Replace the cream with milk. Leave out the watercress, nutmeg and Wensleydale and use a selection of the following:

*12 oz/350g streaky bacon – fried*
*2 chopped onions – sautéed*
*8 oz/225g grated cheese*
*¹/₂ lb/225g spinach – cooked and chopped*

**Serves 6-8.**

# SOUFFLES

........................................................

Soufflés are so easy to make, but the crucial point comes at serving time. Make this when it can be guaranteed that everyone will be ready to eat as soon as the soufflé is cooked. The Aga is ideal for soufflés because the oven is hot, so you get a well risen soufflé that remains moist inside. This is a basic cheese soufflé recipe, but I have given a list of variations at the end.

*2 oz/50g butter*
*2 oz/50g flour*
*¹/₂ pint/300ml milk*
*4 oz/100g grated Gruyère*
*pinch grated nutmeg*
*salt and pepper*
*3 egg yolks and 4 egg whites*

Melt the butter in a saucepan, stir in the flour and cook for 1 minute. Gradually stir in the milk until a thick sauce forms, boil for 3 minutes beating well to make the sauce thick and glossy. Remove from the heat, beat in the cheese, a little salt, pepper, nutmeg and the egg yolks.

Whisk the egg whites until stiff. Fold 1 tablespoon of egg white into the sauce. Gently fold the sauce into the remaining egg whites using a metal spoon. Gently pour into a well buttered 2½ pint (1.500l) soufflé dish. For the 2-oven Aga, put the oven shelf on the floor of the roasting oven and slide in the soufflé. Put the cold shelf on the second set of runners down. For the 4-oven Aga, put the oven shelf on the bottom set of runners of the baking oven and slide in the soufflé. Bake for 20-25 minutes until the soufflé is risen, with a high golden crown. Serve at once.

## VARIATIONS
Replace the cheese with one of the following:
*•4 oz/100g finely chopped ham*
*•4oz/100g finely flaked smoked mackerel*
*•4 oz/100g finely chopped, fried mushrooms*
*• 8 oz/200g cooked finely chopped spinach and 2 oz/100g grated*
*Gruyère and a pinch of nutmeg.*

**Serves 4.**
........................................................

..........

# PASTA WITH ASPARAGUS AND PARMESAN

........................................................

*1 onion – finely chopped*
*14 oz/400g thin asparagus*
*2 oz/50g butter*
*3 fl oz/90ml dry white wine*
*14 oz/400g dried pasta shapes (penne or spirals)*
*10 fl oz/284ml extra thick double cream*
*salt and pepper*
*2 oz/50g Parmesan cheese – grated*

Cut the asparagus into 2-inch/5cm lengths, and blanch them in boiling water for 2-3 minutes until tender. Reserve 5 tablespoons of the blanching water.

Melt the butter in a saucepan on the simmering plate. Cook the onion until soft. Add the asparagus, pour in the reserved blanching water and the wine. Cook until most of the liquid has evaporated.

Cook the pasta on the boiling plate in plenty of boiling, salted water until *al dente*. Drain.

Add the cream to the sauce and stir well. Heat gently until bubbling. Stir in half the cheese, taste and season.

Toss the sauce into the pasta. Serve with the remaining Parmesan sprinkled over.

**Serves 4-6.**
........................................................

# JACKET OR BAKED POTATOES

Jacket potatoes baked in the Aga bear no resemblance to potatoes baked in the microwave oven or even in some gas and electric ovens. They have a crisp "jacket" and a fluffy middle. Choose maincrop potatoes of an even size so that they cook evenly together. The fluffiness of the inside will depend upon the variety chosen. Scrub the potatoes well. Cut a cross in the middle to slit the skin and prevent bursting. I find that at the end of the cooking the potato can be squeezed on the bottom and the cross opens up. This is lovely with a knob of butter or a dollop of soured cream. The potatoes can also be scooped out after baking, the inside forked together with a variety of fillings and returned to the shell. Heat through again. Serve with salad for a complete meal.

To bake the potatoes: place the prepared potatoes directly on the oven shelf. Have the shelf on the third set of runners from the top in the roasting oven. Bake for approximately 1 hour – this time will vary according to the size of the potatoes chosen.

FILLING IDEAS:
- *grated cheese*
- *cottage cheese*
- *diced ham*
- *crispy diced bacon*
- *tuna fish and mayonnaise*
- *sweetcorn and chives*
- *beaten egg and cheese*

# OVEN CHIPS

........................................................

These are a cross between baked potatoes and shop-bought oven chips. They have a good flavour and can be as crispy as you like.

*1 lb/450g maincrop potatoes – scrubbed*
*1 tbsp olive oil*
*salt*

Heat the oil in the small roasting tin.

Slice the potatoes into fingers, about eight for each potato, and toss in the oil. Sprinkle on a little salt.

Hang the tin from the top set of runners in the roasting oven. Cook for half an hour. Stir round to re-coat with the oil. Cook for a further 20-30 minutes – move the tin down the oven if they are browning too much.

The cooking time will vary according to the type of potato used.

Serve with turkey burgers, grilled meat or fish. Sprinkle with sea salt before serving.

**Serves 4.**
........................................................

# ROSTI

.................................................

This classic Swiss dish is a popular way of serving potatoes. Serve with thin slices of Emmental or Gruyère and a side salad for a complete meal.

*2¹/₂ lb/1kg waxy potatoes*
*salt and pepper*
*2 oz/50g butter*
*2 tbsp oil*

Wash the potatoes. Try to have the potatoes roughly the same size so that they cook evenly.

Place them in a saucepan of boiling water. Cover and move to the simmering oven for 20-30 minutes until the potatoes are just tender – this will depend on the size of the potatoes and the type. Drain and put to one side to cool. This can be done the day before they are needed.

Peel and coarsely grate the potatoes, seasoning with salt and pepper.

Heat half the butter and oil in a heavy frying pan on the boiling plate and press the potatoes in to make a cake.

Cook for 10-15 minutes, transferring to the simmering plate if too hot, until the bottom is golden and crusty.

Invert the rosti onto a plate. Heat the rest of the butter and oil in the pan, slide the rosti back into the pan and cook the second side for about 10 minutes.

Serve hot cut into wedges.

**Serves 4.**
.................................................

# ROAST MEDITERRANEAN VEGETABLES

I find this a quick and easy method of cooking vegetables like aubergines and courgettes, and it really brings out their fresh flavour. Serve them hot or cold tossed in French dressing, or even layer them up after cooking, to make a vegetarian lasagne. Add tomatoes, roughly chopped, for the last 10 minutes to make a ratatouille.

## A SELECTION TO SUIT THE SEASON OR YOUR TASTE:

- *aubergine*
- *courgette*
- *red pepper*
- *yellow pepper*
- *shallots*
- *olive oil*
- *sea salt*

Dice the vegetables into roughly 1-inch cubes. Place in the small roasting tin. Toss in 1-2 tablespoons of olive oil, just to coat. The amount of oil will vary according to the amount of vegetables. Toss with a little sea salt.

Slide the roasting tin onto the top set of runners of the roasting oven.

Roast the vegetables for 20-30 minutes until cooked but still firm.

# CRUMBED TOMATOES

..................................................

This is a good winter vegetable standby to serve with chops instead of a sauce.

*2 medium onions*
*2 oz/50g butter*
*2 x 14oz/400g cans tomatoes*
*6 oz/175g breadcrumbs*
*1 tsp parsley – chopped*
*finely grated rind of $^1/_2$ a lemon*
*salt and pepper*

Peel and finely slice the onions. Melt 1 oz/25g butter in a pan and stir in the onions. Cook slowly until golden brown. Spoon into a shallow, oven-proof dish.

Halve or quarter the tomatoes and pour over the onions, with the tomato juice.

Mix the breadcrumbs with the parsley, lemon rind, salt and pepper and scatter over the tomatoes. Dot with shavings of the remaining 1 oz/25g butter.

Bake in the roasting oven with the shelf on the floor of the oven for 30 minutes until bubbling hot and crisp on top.

**Serves 4-6.**
..................................................

# PEPERONATA

..................................................

This is the most tasty way I know of cooking peppers and it looks most attractive. Cut the peppers and tomatoes to similar shapes and sizes to make the finished dish look its best.

*6 small peppers, assorted colours*
*4 tbsp olive oil*
*2 onions, skinned and finely sliced*
*1 clove garlic, skinned and crushed*
*1 lb/450g plum tomatoes, skinned, quartered and seeded*
*2 tbsp balsamic vinegar*
*10-12 black olives, pitted and halved*
*salt and pepper*

Wash, quarter and de-seed the peppers.

Heat the oil in a large cast-iron pan on the floor of the roasting oven. Stir in the onions and cook for about 5 minutes until soft. Add the garlic and peppers, stir occasionally and cook for 10-15 minutes until the peppers are softening.

Stir in the tomatoes and cook again for 5-10 more minutes. Stir in the vinegar, salt and pepper and olives.

Serve hot or cold.

**This will serve 8 as a starter with crusty bread or 4-6 as an accompaniment to a main meal.**
..................................................

# STUFFED TOMATOES

......................................................

These tomatoes make a good starter for eight or a light lunch dish for four. The baking seems to bring out the sweet flavour of the tomatoes. Prepare in advance and bake when needed.

*4 large beefsteak tomatoes*
*salt and pepper*
*3 tbsp parsley – chopped*
*2 tbsp basil – chopped*
*6 tbsp grated Sbrinz or Parmesan*
*6 tbsp fresh breadcrumbs*
*1 tbsp olive oil*

Cut the tomatoes in half horizontally. Scoop out most of the insides, using a sharp teaspoon or grapefruit knife.

Mix together the parsley, basil, 4 tablespoons of grated cheese, salt and pepper and breadcrumbs. Fill the tomatoes with the stuffing. Stand in a lightly oiled oven-proof dish.

Put the oven shelf on the floor of the roasting oven. Put in the tomatoes and bake for 20 minutes or until golden brown and the tomatoes are softened.

Sprinkle on the remaining cheese and serve with warm crusty bread.

**Serves 4 for lunch or 8 for starters**
......................................................

# MUSHROOM RISOTTO

This is a delicious dish for anyone who loves mushrooms. 4 oz/100g crisply cooked bacon can be added at the end if you are not cooking for a vegetarian. Dried *porcini* mushrooms can be soaked in water for half an hour and used if fresh varieties are not available. Use the soaking liquid for cooking the risotto.

*4 oz/100g assorted wild mushrooms – sliced*
*1 medium onion – chopped*
*2 tbsp olive oil*
*2 oz/50g butter*
*1 clove garlic – finely chopped*
*1-1½ pints/600-900ml light stock – hot*
*10 oz/275g risotto rice*
*8 tbsp white wine*
*2 oz/50g finely grated Sbrinz or Parmesan*

Fry the onion in the oil and half the butter in a deep frying pan on the simmering plate until soft and pale gold. Stir in the garlic and the mushrooms.

Stir in the rice until well coated with the butter, add the wine and boil for about 2 minutes until it is absorbed. Gradually add the stock, stirring, until it is all absorbed and the rice is cooked, about 10-15 minutes. The rice should not become soggy and should have a little sauce round it – you may not need all the stock.

Remove from the heat, stir in the butter and most of the cheese. Taste and season. Serve with the remaining grated cheese.

**Serves 4.**

# MIXED RICE PILAFF

Wild rice is expensive, but a small amount mixed with brown rice will add flavour and texture as well as enhance the appearance. Serve this pilaff with a casserole.

*12 oz/350g long-grain brown rice*
*2 oz/50g wild rice*
*4 tbsp olive oil*
*salt and pepper*
*2 oz/50g pine kernels – toasted*

Measure the washed rice into a saucepan, add 1½ times as much water and a good pinch of salt. Bring to the boil on the boiling plate. Cover with a lid and transfer to the simmering oven. Cook for about 20 minutes, until the rice is cooked and most of the water absorbed. Drain well.

Stir the oil into the drained, warm rice. Stir in the toasted pine kernels and adjust the seasoning.

**Serves 6.**

# MIXED VEGETABLE RING

..............................................

This recipe came about because I needed a quick vegetarian supper dish. Choux pastry baked in the Aga is deliciously puffy and moist. I have also used this recipe with 4 oz/100g prawns stirred in for non-vegetarians.

### RING
Follow the recipe as for Gougère (see page 35) to end of third paragraph.

Grease a baking tray. Spoon out tablespoons of the mixture into a circle. Bake in the roasting oven with the shelf on the third set of runners from the top. Check after 15 minutes; if it is browning move down with the shelf on the floor of the oven. Bake for a further 20-30 minutes until risen, puffy and golden brown.

### FILLING
*1 oz/25g butter*
*1 large onion – chopped*
*1 clove garlic – crushed*
*2 oz/50g mushrooms – sliced*
*2 courgettes – finely sliced*
*1 small aubergine – diced*
*1 red pepper – seeded and sliced*
*3 tomatoes – skinned and chopped*
*salt and pepper*

Melt the butter in a saucepan, stir in the onion and cook until softened. Stir in the remaining ingredients, and cover with a lid. Bring to simmering point on the simmering plate, taking care not to burn. Transfer to the simmering oven for 45 minutes until the vegetables are cooked but not mushy.

Place the choux ring on a large oven-proof plate, and spoon the vegetable filling into the centre. If liked, pop into the roasting oven for 5-10 minutes until piping hot.

Serve immediately with a side salad and crusty bread.

**Serves 4.**

..............................................

..............

# BROCCOLI QUICHE

I found this recipe persuaded my children to eat green vegetables because of the thin layer of tomato ketchup in the base!

*8 oz/225g shortcrust pastry*
*8 oz/225g Broccoli florets*
*2 tbsp tomato ketchup*
*3 eggs*
*¹/₂ pint/300ml milk*
*salt and pepper*
*4 oz/100g Gruyère – grated*

Line a 9-inch/23-cm flan dish with the shortcrust pastry. Cook the broccoli in a small amount of boiling, salted water until crisp and still bright green. Drain.

Spread the ketchup over the base of the pastry case. Scatter the drained broccoli florets over the ketchup.

Beat together the eggs, milk, salt and pepper and half the grated cheese and pour over the broccoli. Sprinkle on the remaining cheese. Bake on the floor of the roasting oven for 30 minutes, until the quiche is golden brown and set.

Serves 6.

# COURGETTE TART

········································

This is a good way to use up courgettes in the summer and a good vegetarian dish.

*½ lb/225g shortcrust pastry*
*1 onion – chopped*
*2 tbsp olive oil*
*4-6 small courgettes – finely sliced*
*salt and pepper*
*4 eggs*
*½ pint/300ml single cream*
*¼ pint/150ml milk*
*freshly grated nutmeg*
*4 oz/100g Gruyère – grated*

Roll out the pastry to line a 9 or 10-inch/23 or 25-cm flan dish. Fry the onion gently in the olive oil until soft. Remove with a slotted spoon to the pastry case.

Fry the courgettes until golden brown. Remove to the pastry case.

Beat the eggs, add the milk, cream, salt and pepper and the nutmeg. Pour this mixture over the courgettes and sprinkle over the grated Gruyère.

Bake on the floor of the roasting oven for about 30 minutes until the tart is set in the middle and golden brown.

Serves 6.

········································

# BEAN AND TOMATO CASSEROLE

....................................................

This is a filling dish, lovely on its own or with a green salad.

*3 oz/75g red kidney beans*
*3 oz/75g black-eyed beans*
*3 oz/75g butter beans*
*1 large onion – chopped*
*2 sticks celery – chopped*
*2 tbsp oil*
*1 clove garlic – crushed*
*1 x 14oz/400g can tomatoes – chopped*
*¼ pint/150ml light stock*
*1/4 tsp chilli powder*
*salt and pepper*
*3 oz/75g wholemeal breadcrumbs*
*4 oz/100g tasty cheese – grated*

Soak the beans in water overnight. Drain and place them in a large saucepan. Cover with water, bring to the boil and boil rapidly for 10-15 minutes. Cover and transfer to the simmering oven for 1-3 hours, until all the beans are tender. Drain and rinse.

Heat the oil in a pan and cook the onion and celery until they begin to soften. Add the garlic and fry until soft. Stir in the tomatoes and stock, chilli powder, beans, salt and pepper to taste. Bring to the boil, cover and transfer to the simmering oven for 30-40 minutes. Transfer to an oven-proof dish. Mix the breadcrumbs and cheese and scatter over the bean mixture. Place in the middle of the roasting oven for 10-15 minutes until golden brown and crusty.

**Serves 4.**
....................................................

# LENTIL RISSOLES

.................................................

These tasty rissoles are a good introduction to lentils for anyone who is a devoted meat eater. Serve with home-made tomato sauce.

*2 tbsp oil*
*1 onion – finely chopped*
*2 sticks celery – chopped*
*2 carrots – finely diced*
*8 oz/225g orange lentils – washed and picked over*
*1 pint/600ml water*
*1 tsp ground coriander*
*2 tbsp parsley – chopped*
*6 oz/175g wholemeal breadcrumbs*
*2 tbsp flour*
*1 egg – beaten*
*salt and pepper*

Heat the oil in a saucepan, add the onion, celery and carrot and cook until softened. Stir in the lentils, water, coriander and salt and pepper. Bring to the boil, cover and transfer to the simmering oven for 1-1½ hours until the lentils are cooked and the liquid has been absorbed.

Mix in the parsley and 2 oz/50g of the breadcrumbs. Turn the mixture onto a plate and allow to cool for a little.

Using floured hands, shape the mixture into rissoles or cakes. Dip in the beaten egg and then in the remaining breadcrumbs.

Either fry in a little oil in a frying pan on the top of the Aga, or heat oil in a roasting tin on the floor of the Aga. Fry the rissoles until crisp and golden on both sides.

Makes 8 rissoles.
.................................................

# YORKSHIRE PUDDING

A Yorkshire pudding is neither a vegetable nor a vegetarian meal, yet it finds itself in this section, unwanted by any other, but wonderful nevertheless. Yorkshire puddings need a good, hot oven to make them puff up, so to overcome the problem of slightly low heat at the end of the roast cooking time, I cook my Yorkshire puddings before the meat goes in the oven. Yes, it does work! Cook the puddings in the usual way. When fully cooked, remove them and put them to one side. When the joint is removed for resting before carving, return the puddings to the roasting oven to heat through.

*4 oz/100g plain flour*
*pinch salt*
*1 egg*
*¹/₂ pint/300ml milk*
*a little lard or dripping*

Sieve the flour and salt into a basin. Make a well in the centre and crack in the egg. Beat the egg with a wooden spoon, gradually drawing in the flour. Slowly add the milk, beating the batter well until a smooth, creamy batter has been made.

Place a little lard or dripping into the base of 8 little bun tins.

Put the oven shelf on the second set of runners from the top and put in the tray. Leave until the fat is melted and hazy hot.

Remove from the oven and pour in the batter. Return to the oven and cook until risen and crisp and golden brown, about 25-30 minutes.

**Makes 8 bun-size puddings.**

# PUDDINGS

# CREME CARAMEL

......................................................

This popular dish can be served as a light dessert, made in advance to allow for chilling and the flavours to develop. This recipe serves six, either made in one soufflé dish, or in individual ramekin dishes.

### CARAMEL
*4 oz/100g granulated sugar*
*3 tbsp water*

### CUSTARD
*4 eggs*
*1 pint/600ml milk*
*3 oz/75g caster sugar*
*a few drops of vanilla essence*

Put the sugar for the caramel in a clean, dry saucepan. If you are making individual ramekins, you may like to use an ounce or two more of sugar. Stand the pan on the simmering plate and heat gently to dissolve the sugar, heating until it turns to a caramel colour. Keep an eye on it! Remove from the heat and stir in the water to stop the caramel cooking further – but take care, it may spatter your hand. Return the pan to the simmering plate and stir until a thick caramel sauce is formed. Pour the sauce into the dish or ramekins.

Lightly whisk the eggs with the vanilla essence. Pour the milk and sugar into a saucepan and heat gently on the simmering plate, just until the sugar is dissolved. Pour onto the eggs and beat well. Strain the mixture through a sieve into a jug. Pour over the prepared caramel.

Stand the dish or ramekins in the small roasting pan. Pour boiling water around the dishes to come about half-way up the sides of the roasting pan. Cover with a sheet of foil.

Slide the tin onto the bottom set of runners of the roasting oven for 20 minutes. Transfer the tin to the floor of the simmering oven for 30 minutes to 1 hour, until the custard is completely set. Leave to cool, and chill before turning out.

**Serves 6.**
......................................................

# STEAMED PUDDINGS

Steamed puddings are marvellous when cooked in the Aga, and the kitchen does not fill with steam. I am giving the recipe for a fairly basic steamed pudding and several variations; you may, of course, want to try your own. These old-fashioned puddings are becoming popular again because of their flavour and though, with modern eating trends, we may not revert to this sort of pudding daily, it is great for a treat. I find a steamed pudding good for a supper party because it can be left cooking slowly in the simmering oven, even if guests are late or we are lingering over the main course.

*6 oz/175g self-raising flour*
*pinch salt*
*4 oz/100g butter or soft margarine*
*4 oz/100g caster sugar*
*2 eggs*

Grease well a 2-pint/1.1 litre pudding basin. The plastic boilable ones with a lid are useful. Spoon your topping choice into the bottom of the basin.

Beat together the flour, salt, butter, sugar and eggs to a soft consistency. If it is very dry, especially with wholemeal flour, beat in a little milk. Carefully spoon the mixture into the prepared basin.

Cover with a circle of greaseproof paper and either a sheet of pleated foil or the plastic lid.

Use a deep enough saucepan to take the pudding basin standing on a trivet, an old saucer or a wad of newspaper. Stand the pudding in the pan on the trivet. Pour in enough boiling water to come half-way up the basin and cover the pan. Stand it on the simmering plate, bring to the boil and simmer (if necessary move slightly off the plate) for 30 minutes. Remove to the simmering oven and leave for about 3 hours. The pudding will continue to steam – the water should not need topping up. Turn out onto a warm plate and serve with cream, yoghurt, custard or more topping as a sauce.

**Serves 6.**

## VARIATION

## CHOCOLATE AND BRAZIL NUT

*3 tbsp cocoa*
*2 oz/50g brazil nuts*

Add 3 tbsp cocoa, sifted with the flour, to the basic mixture. Chop the nuts and fold into the mixture before putting in the basin.

## TOPPINGS

### 1. STICKY TOFFEE PUDDING

*7 oz/200g soft brown sugar*
*4 oz/100g butter*
*6 tbsp double cream*

Place all the ingredients in a small saucepan and stir over gentle heat to melt the butter and dissolve the sugar. Bring to the boil and simmer for 3 minutes. Pour into the basin before adding the sponge mixture.

### 2. MARMALADE

*3 tbsp marmalade*

Put the marmalade into the bottom of the basin.

### 3. SYRUP

*3 tbsp golden syrup*

Put the warmed syrup into the bottom of the basin.

# PAVLOVA

.................................................

This is always a popular dessert for a special meal. I make my meringues dry so that they can be made in advance and stored, either in a box in the freezer or a dry cupboard. I can also fill them an hour or two before serving, which allows time for the cream and filling to soften the meringue slightly and me time to get on with other preparations.

*3 egg whites*
*6 oz/175g caster sugar or 4 oz/100g caster sugar and*
*2 oz/50g soft brown sugar*
*1 tsp white wine vinegar and 1 tsp cornflour blended together*

Prepare a baking tray, line with non-stick parchment or a re-usable, non-stick baking tray. Whisk the egg whites in a clean, dry and grease-free bowl until white and fluffy. Continue to whisk, adding the sugar 1 teaspoonful at a time. When all the sugar is in, whisk in the cornflour mixture.

Using tablespoons, spoon the meringue into a circle. Use some meringue to fill in the circle, but ensure the sides are higher than the base. Roughen the edges. Bake in the simmering oven on the bottom set of runners for 2 hours. Remove from the baking sheet and stand upside down on the sheet. Return to the oven, leaving the door slightly ajar. I continue to dry overnight or at least for 6 hours. Remove from the oven and allow to cool before wrapping and storing or filling with cream.

### Serves 6.
.................................................

### FILLING

*¹/₂ pint/300ml double or whipping cream*
*8 oz/225g fresh fruit e.g. raspberries, strawberries, kiwi fruit, passion fruit*

In winter I sometimes fold 2 tablespoons of chopped stem ginger and 1 tablespoon of ginger syrup into the cream. Alternatively frozen fruit selections can be stirred into the cream, but drain off the juices first. Whip the cream to a soft peak. Gently fold in half the prepared fruit. Pile this into the middle of the meringue and decorate with the remaining fruit.

..........

# RICE PUDDING

......................................................

I always think that the Aga would be the ideal cooker for rice pudding, cooked slowly, but I can honestly say that this is the dish that has caused me most problems with my Aga; and judging by the talk at my Aga days, other people share these problems. I know, from testing, that the use of semi-skimmed milk will not work. So no low-fat rice puddings – the more cream, the better! If you have a little cream left over, stir it in with the milk for a creamier pudding. Timing will be an estimate because all the ovens vary and we all like our puddings cooked to a different degree of thickness.

*1 pint/600ml full-fat milk*
*1 oz/25g round-grain pudding rice*
*1 oz/25g sugar*

Put the rice and sugar in a buttered, oven-proof dish. Pour in the milk. Have the oven shelf on the flour of the roasting oven. Put the pudding in the oven for 15 minutes. Stir in any skin forming – this makes a creamier pudding. Return the pudding to the oven and again cook for 15 minutes and then stir in any skin.

For a 2-oven Aga, slide in the cold shelf on the third set of runners from the top. For a 4-oven Aga, transfer the pudding to the baking oven, where the shelf is on the bottom set of runners.

Time the pudding for a further ½ – 1 hour; take care that it does not boil over. If the pudding wants to boil over and is not thick enough for your taste, open the skin to let out hot air.

**Serves 4.**

......................................................

# BREAD AND BUTTER PUDDING

......................................................

This is an old-fashioned pudding that is popular again. Cooked gently in a bain-marie in the simmering oven, the custard will be just set and smooth. Before starting, check that your dish will fit in the roasting tin.

*3 bread rolls or brioche slices*
*1 oz/25g butter*
*¹/₄ oz sultanas (soaked in water for ¹/₂ hour and then drained)*
*8 fl oz/225ml milk*
*1 vanilla pod*
*8 fl oz/225ml Greek-style yoghurt*
*4 eggs*
*3 oz/75g caster sugar*
*a little icing sugar*
*pinch of salt*

Cut rolls into thin slices and spread with butter. Arrange in a buttered dish and sprinkle with sultanas. Bring the milk, salt and vanilla pod to the boil.

Gently stir in the yoghurt and mix well. Mix the eggs and caster sugar together. Add the milk and yoghurt and mix well. Strain and pour over the bread.

Stand the dish in the roasting tin. Pour hot water round the dish to about half way up the side of the dish. Slide the roasting tin into the roasting oven on the bottom set of runners and bake for 10 minutes.

Transfer roasting tin to simmering oven for 30-45 minutes until set.

Sieve over a little icing sugar and serve warm.

**Serves 6-8.**
......................................................

# APPLE AND ALMOND CRUMBLE

......................................................

This is a slightly unusual crumble, the Amaretti biscuits provide an almond flavour with a slightly different texture. Eating apples have been used, which means that no extra sugar is needed and they cook until soft but still holding their shape.

*6 crisp eating apples*
*juice of 1 lemon*
*2 oz/50g Amaretti biscuits, about 8*
*4 oz/100g plain flour*
*1 oz/25g soft brown sugar*
*¹/₂ level tsp ground cinnamon*
*3 oz/75g softened butter*

Peel, quarter, core and thickly slice the apples. Toss in the lemon juice. Tip into an oven-proof dish.

Roughly crumble the Amaretti. Mix with the flour, sugar and cinnamon. Rub in the butter until crumbly and just beginning to hold together. Spoon over the apples.

Bake with the oven shelf on the floor of the roasting oven for the 2-oven Aga, baking oven for the 4-oven Aga. This takes about 45 minutes. If, after about 20 minutes in the roasting oven, the top is browning too much, either cover with foil or slide in the cold shelf. The apples should be soft when prodded.

**Serves 4.**
......................................................

# MAGIC LEMON PUDDING

........................................................

I have been making this pudding for years, it is so popular. Now my children make it, they never cease to wonder how the sauce starts on the top and ends up at the bottom!

### SPONGE
*4 oz/100g self-raising flour*
*4 oz/100g butter*
*4 oz/100g caster sugar*
*2 eggs*
*grated rind of 1 lemon*
*1-2 tbsp milk*

### SAUCE
*4 oz/100g caster sugar*
*2 tbsp cornflour*
*juice of 1 lemon made up to ¹/₂ pint/300ml with boiling water*

Grease a 2 pint oven-proof dish. Combine the flour, softened butter, sugar, eggs and lemon rind in a mixing bowl. Beat together with an electric beater or wooden spoon until smooth and fluffy. Add milk to make a soft, dropping consistency if needed. Spread into prepared dish. For the sauce, combine the sugar and cornflour. Gradually blend in the lemon juice and boiling water mixture. Pour onto the sponge mixture. For the 2-oven Aga, have the oven shelf on the floor of the roasting oven. Stand the sponge dish on the shelf, slide the cold shelf above, allowing room for the mixture to rise. For the 4-oven Aga, put the oven shelf on the bottom set of runners and put in the pudding. Bake for 25-35 minutes – this depends upon the depth of the dish. When baked, the mixture should be golden and firm on the top. The sauce will now be at the bottom. Serve hot with yoghurt or cream.

**Serves 4.**

### MAGIC CHOCOLATE PUDDING
Replace the lemon rind with 1 tablesepoon cocoa powder in the sponge mixture and replace the lemon juice with 1 tablespoon cocoa powder, again made up to ¹/₂pint/300ml with the boiling water, for the sauce.

........

105

# QUICK CLAFOUTIS

...............................................

This is a standby pudding using store-cupboard ingredients. Other types of canned fruit can be used — apricots give a more tangy taste.

*1 x 14¹/₂oz/410g can peach slices*
*1 level tbsp self-raising flour*
*2 eggs – beaten*
*1 x 15 oz/425g can or carton of custard*
*1 tsp caster sugar*

Butter a shallow oven-proof dish and dust with the caster sugar. Drain the peaches, pat dry with kitchen paper, arrange in the prepared dish. Beat the flour and eggs together, whisk in the custard. Pour over the peaches and level the surface.

Put the oven shelf on the third set of runners from the top of the roasting oven, put in the clafoutis and bake for 30 minutes until risen and golden brown. Dust with caster sugar and serve immediately.

**Serves 4.**
...............................................

# CHRISTMAS PUDDING

......................................................

This is sugar-free Christmas pudding, not that anyone except the cook would know! There is so much fruit in a Christmas pudding that no extra sugar is needed. However, it does mean that this recipe does not have the keeping quality of a sugar-rich pudding. Keep it in the fridge for 2 weeks or freeze. I use plastic basins with lids, so there is no danger of the fruit attacking the aluminium dish during storage. This recipe makes one large pudding.

*2 oz/50g currants*
*3 oz/75g raisins*
*3 oz/75g sultanas*
*2 oz/50g candied peel – chopped*
*2 oz/50g stoned dates – chopped*
*5 fl oz/150ml Guinness*
*1 oz/25g almonds – shredded*
*1 small cooking apple – grated*
*1 medium carrot – grated*
*1¹/₂ oz/35g fresh breadcrumbs*
*2 oz/50g vegetable suet or margarine – melted*
*¹/₂ tsp baking powder*
*pinch salt*
*¹/₄ tsp nutmeg – freshly grated*
*¹/₂ tsp ground cinnamon*
*1 egg – beaten*
*4 tbsp brandy*

Grease a 1¹/₂-2 pint/900-1200ml pudding basin.

Put the currants, raisins, sultanas, peel, dates and Guinness into a bowl, stir, cover and leave to stand somewhere cool for 24 hours. Add the almonds, cooking apple and carrot and stir well. Add the breadcrumbs, suet or margarine, baking powder, spices, salt, egg and brandy. Stir really well – let the whole family have a stir and a wish.

Put the mixture into the greased pudding basin. Press down and smooth the top. Cover with a circle of greaseproof paper and put on the lid or foil.

Have a pan large enough to take the pudding standing on a trivet, an old saucer or a wad of newspaper. Put the pudding in, half fill the pan with water and bring to boiling point. On the simmering plate, simmer for 30 minutes. Put the oven shelf on the floor of the simmering oven and put the pan in for 12 hours or overnight. Remove from the pan and cool. Cover with fresh greaseproof paper and foil, if using, before storing.

On Christmas Day: stand basin in a pan as above, pour water half-way up the side of the basin, bring to the boil and then simmer for half an hour. Transfer to the simmering oven for 2-3 hours. Allow to stand at room temperature for half an hour before turning out onto a warmed plate. Serve with cream.

**Makes 1 large pudding.**

# FRUIT FLAN – FRENCH STYLE

Do you admire the pretty French flans both in our supermarkets and in France? They are not difficult to make and are much tastier when freshly baked. Supermarkets are now selling excellent fresh or frozen pastry.

*8 oz/225g rich shortcrust pastry*

### FILLING
*2 egg yolks*
*2¹/₂ oz caster sugar*
*³/₄ oz/20g flour*
*¹/₄ pint/150ml milk*
*few drops vanilla essence*
*mixed fruits eg strawberries, kiwi, peaches, pineapples*
*3-4 tbsp apricot or strawberry conserve – sieved and warm*

Roll out the pastry to fit a 13 x 4 x 1-inch/34 x 11-cm flan tin or a 9-inch round flan tin. Chill.

To make the filling, cream the egg yolks and sugar until light and fluffy. Mix in the flour and milk. Cook over a gentle heat, stirring until thickened. Stir in vanilla essence and cool.

Bake the pastry case. Prick the base well. Bake on the floor of the roasting oven for 6-8 minutes until crisp and golden brown. Cool.

Remove the pastry case from the tin and stand on a plate. Fill with crème pâtissière.

Decorate with sliced fruits and glaze with the conserve.

Makes 1 large flan.

# FUDGE NUT TRANCHE

..............................................

An ideal winter pudding for nut lovers, this flan is made in a tranche tin. It is easy to slice, making it particularly useful for the buffet table.

### PASTRY
*4 oz/100g butter*
*6 oz/175g plain flour*
*1 oz/25g caster sugar*
*2-3 tbsp water*

### FILLING
*4 oz/100g butter*
*4 oz/100g skinned hazelnuts*
*4 oz/100g pecan nuts*
*3 oz/75g soft brown sugar*
*5 fl oz double cream*
*rind and juice of 1 lemon*
*1 egg – beaten*
*6 oz/175g mixed whole nuts eg brazils, walnuts, hazelnuts*
*2 tbsp warm apricot jam*

Rub butter into flour and stir in the sugar. Bind together with 2-3 tablespoons of water. Roll dough to line a 14 x 4-inch/34 x 11-cm tranche tin.

Toast the hazelnuts and pecans until lightly browned on a baking tray towards the top of the roasting oven. Cool and chop roughly.

Cream the butter and sugar, stir in chopped nuts, the finely grated lemon rind, 2 tablespoons of the lemon juice, and the beaten egg. Beat in the cream. Pour into the flan case and arrange whole nuts on top.

Bake on the floor of the roasting oven for 25-30 minutes until set.

Brush flan evenly with warm apricot jam.

**Serves 6-8.**
..............................................

# LEMON AND WALNUT TART

The lemon in this recipe complements the richness of the walnuts. Serve with cream or a citrus sauce.

*1 sweet pastry case – 9 inch/23cm round or oblong*
*4 oz/100g butter*
*4 oz/100g soft brown sugar*
*2 level tbsp self-raising flour*
*3 oz/75g chopped walnuts*
*2 eggs – separated*
*rind and juice of 1 lemon*

Cream butter and sugar until light and fluffy. Beat in the flour, walnuts, egg yolks, lemon rind and juice. Whisk egg whites until stiff, and fold them in. Pour into flan case and bake on the floor of the roasting oven for 45 minutes until golden and risen. Serve with cream or citrus sauce.

**Serves 6-8.**

# CITRUS SAUCE

........................................................

This is a tangy lemon sauce ideal for serving with a rich pudding such as Lemon and Walnut Tart (see page 111) or a steamed sponge pudding.

*4 level tbsp lemon curd*
*juice and rind of 2 lemons*
*5 fl oz/150ml carton double cream or crème fraîche*
*1 level tsp cornflour*
*1-2 level tbsp icing sugar, sieved*
*water*

Place lemon curd, grated lemon rinds, 4 tablespoons of the lemon juice and 4 tablespoons of water in a small saucepan. Dissolve over gentle heat.

Stir in the cream, bring to the boil and bubble for 2-3 minutes, stirring.

Blend cornflour with 2 teaspoons of cold water, whisk into the sauce, and simmer for 2-3 minutes until slightly thickened. Stir in icing sugar to taste.

**Serves 6-8.**

# GERMAN APPLE CAKE

I make this when I have a glut of apples in the autumn. This cake, which cuts into 8 slices, is lovely served with thick cream for a pudding.

### BASE
*4 oz/100g self-raising flour*
*2 oz/50g soft brown sugar*
*2 oz/50g ground almonds*
*3 oz/75g butter*
*1 small egg or ¹/₂ a standard egg, beaten*
*1 tsp lemon juice*

### FILLING
*1 lb/450g cooking apples*
*2 oz/50g soft brown sugar*
*1 tsp lemon juice*

### TOPPING
*2 oz/50g self-raising flour*
*2 oz/50g soft brown sugar*
*1 tsp ground cinnamon*
*2 oz/50g butter*

Grease and base-line an 8-inch/20-cm cake tin. Sieve the flour into a bowl, stir in the sugar and 1 oz/25g ground almonds. Rub in the butter until the mixture is like breadcrumbs. Bind the mixture with the egg and lemon juice. Press into the prepared tin and sprinkle over the remaining 1 oz/25g ground almonds — this will help to absorb the apple juices. Peel and finely slice the apples and toss them in the lemon juice and sugar. Arrange the slices on the base. Sieve together the flour and cinnamon of the topping mixture. Stir in the sugar and rub in the butter. Sprinkle over the apples.

For the 2-oven Aga, have the oven shelf on the floor of the oven and bake the apple cake for half an hour. Then slide the cold shelf in on the second set of runners from the top and bake for a further 30-45 minutes, depending on the apples. They should be soft when prodded with a knife. For the 4-oven Aga, have the oven shelf on the third set of runners from the top of the baking oven and bake for 1 to 1¼ hours, until the apples are soft when prodded with a knife. Cool in the tin. Dust with icing sugar before serving warm or cold.

# CHOCOLATE POTS

These little puddings have a surprise in store. They have a solid top and are creamy underneath. They cook beautifully in the simmering oven. Make them well in advance to allow time to chill.

*3/4 pint/450ml*
*milk*
*finely grated rind of 1 orange*
*6 oz/175g plain chocolate*
*4 egg yolks*
*1 oz/25g caster sugar*

Pour the milk into a saucepan and add the orange rind. Heat it gently on the simmering plate until boiling. Remove from the heat and leave to stand for 1/4 hour. This allows the orange flavour to infuse the milk.

Break the chocolate into a basin and stand it on top of the Aga to melt. Beat in the egg yolks and sugar. Slowly stir in the milk, blending well.

Strain the mixture into a jug and then pour into 6 ramekin dishes.

Stand the dishes in the small roasting tin. Pour round hot water to come half-way up the ramekin dishes. Slide the roasting tin into the middle position of the simmering oven. Cook for 45 minutes or until set firm.

Remove from the roasting tin, cool and then chill.

**Serves 6.**

# APPLE STRUDEL

Homemade strudels are easy to make now that filo pastry is so readily available. This recipe makes one large strudel, but small individual strudels can easily be made.

*1 packet filo pastry*
*2¹/₂ oz/65g fresh breadcrumbs*
*2¹/₄ lbs/1kg apples*
*4 oz/100g soft brown sugar*
*2¹/₂oz/65g sultanas – optional*
*2¹/₂oz/65g chopped nuts – optional*
*1 tsp ground cinnamon*
*3 oz/75g butter – melted*
*2-3 tsp icing sugar*

Unroll the filo pastry and brush each sheet with melted butter. Lay out, layer upon layer, to make a large oblong to fit your largest baking tray or the cold shelf.

Sprinkle the breadcrumbs over the pastry.

Peel, core and thinly slice the apples. Mix together with the sugar, sultanas and nuts (if using) and cinnamon. Spoon onto the pastry sheet leaving a good 6-inch/15-cm border all round. Fold in the short ends and carefully roll the strudel up so that the join is at the bottom.

Brush with any remaining butter. Bake on the bottom set of runners in the roasting oven for 25-30 minutes until brown and crisp and the apples are cooked. Sprinkle over the icing sugar and return to the second set of runners from the top of the roasting oven for 5 minutes until golden brown and glazed.

makes 8-10.

# HOME BAKING

# CAKES AND BISCUITS

# RICH FRUIT CAKE

Rich fruit cakes baked in the Aga are wonderfully moist and evenly cooked. Cakes cooked in the simmering oven can be left overnight, and there is no need to line the cake tin. Two cakes can be baked at a time, one for you and one to give away! Cooking times vary depending on the size of the tin, the quantity of the mixture and the oven heat. However, I find that any cake put in at bedtime and removed first thing in the morning will be evenly cooked and not overdone. If your simmering oven is low on heat give the cake up to 24 hours. This recipe makes enough mixture for a 9-inch/23-cm round tin or an 8-inch/20-cm square tin. You can halve the recipe easily for a 7-inch/8-cm round or a 6-inch/15-cm square tin, or double the recipe for a 12-inch/30-cm round or 11-inch/28-cm square tin. This is useful for a tiered wedding cake.

*1 lb/450g plain flour*
*¹/₂ level tsp salt*
*1 level tsp ground cinnamon*
*1 level tsp ground mixed spice*
*1 lb/450g sultanas – cleaned*
*12 oz/350g currants – cleaned*
*12 oz/350g raisins – cleaned*
*8 oz/225g glacé cherries*
*2 oz/50g walnuts – chopped*
*10 oz/300g butter – softened*
*10 oz/300g soft brown sugar*
*5 eggs*
*2 tbsp black treacle*
*finely grated rind of 1 lemon*
*4 tbsp brandy*

Grease and line the tin with greaseproof paper. Sieve the flour, salt, cinnamon and mixed spice together. Stand the treacle and a tablespoon in a basin on the Aga to warm.

Weigh and pick over the dried fruits. Cut the cherries in half, wash in warm

water and dry. Add to the other fruit. Chop the walnuts and add to fruit.

Crack the eggs into a basin and beat well together.

Place the butter and sugar in a bowl and beat well until light and fluffy. Beat in the eggs, adding a little flour with each addition to prevent curdling. When all the eggs are beaten in stir in the prepared dried fruits. Fold in the flour, the lemon rind and finally the treacle and brandy. Spoon into the prepared tin and level the top. Place the oven shelf on the floor of the simmering oven, put the cake in and bake for 8-12 hours.

To test when the cake is done, insert a warm skewer into the middle of the cake. If it is cooked, it will come out clean. Cool in the tin. When cold, wrap the cake in foil and store in a cool place.

# SIMNEL CAKE

A traditional Easter or mid-Lent Sunday cake. The marzipan in the middle leaves the cake moist and more-ish.

*8 oz/225g plain flour*
*1 level tsp baking powder*
*1¹/₂ level tsp mixed spice*
*3 eggs*
*6 oz/175g butter*
*6 oz/175g caster or soft brown sugar*
*8 oz/225g sultanas*
*6 oz/175g currants*
*2 oz/50g cut mixed peel*
*2 oz/50g glacé cherries, halved and washed*
*3 tbsp milk*
*12 oz/350g marzipan*
*4-6 oz/100-175g icing sugar*
*1 tbsp apricot jam*
*Easter decorations eg sugar eggs, small chickens etc*

Grease and line an 8-inch/20-cm round, deep cake tin. Roll out 4 oz/100g marzipan to a circle the size of the tin. Sieve together the flour, spice and baking

powder. Beat the eggs together.

Cream together the butter and sugar. Beat in the eggs, a little at a time, with 1 tablespoon of flour. Fold in the remaining flour and stir in the fruit. Add milk if necessary, but do not have the mixture too soft.

Place half the mixture in the cake tin. Level the top the place the marzipan circle over it. Spread the remaining cake mixture on top and level it. Bake.

## BAKING THE SIMNEL CAKE

The cake may be baked either in the roasting oven, in an Aga cake baker, or in an ordinary cake tin in the simmering oven. For the 4-oven Aga, use the baking oven.

**THE CAKE BAKER:** Heat the empty outer container in the roasting oven with the oven shelf on the floor of the oven. Place the cake tin in the trivet, place in the cake baker, return to the oven for 1½ hours. The cake should be evenly baked and slightly shrunk from the sides of the tin.

**THE SIMMERING OVEN:** Place the cake in the oven with the shelf on the bottom set of runners. Bake for 10-12 hours or overnight, until the cake is an even, golden colour and slightly shrunk from the sides of the tin.

**FOUR-OVEN BAKING OVEN:** Put the oven shelf on the floor of the baking oven and bake the cake for 1-1½ hours until the cake is golden brown and slightly shrunk from the sides of the tin. Cool in the tin.

## DECORATING THE SIMNEL CAKE

Remove the greaseproof paper. Brush the top of the cake with the warmed apricot jam.

Divide the marzipan into eleven even-sized pieces. Roll into balls and place around the outside edge of the cake. Flatten tops and press on the cake firmly so that the balls are touching. Make up a thick glacé icing with the icing sugar and boiled water. Pour into the centre of the marzipan decoration.

When the icing is dry decorate with the eggs, chicks or flowers. Tie a yellow ribbon around the cake.

# CHERRY CAKE

........................................................

I like to make this cake in a loaf tin and serve in slices, to show off the glossy cherries. Do not be tempted to mix the cherries in with a food processor or mixer, they will be chopped and won't look so attractive. If necessary fold in with a spatula at the end of mixing before putting in the tin.

*8 oz/225g plain flour*
*1¹/₂ tsp baking powder*
*¹/₄ tsp cream of tartar*
*pinch salt*
*4 oz/100g glacé cherries*
*6 oz/175g butter*
*6 oz/175g caster sugar*
*3 eggs*
*1 tbsp milk*
*¹/₂ tsp vanilla essence*

Grease and base-line an 8-inch/20-cm round tin, or a 2lb/1kg loaf tin. Cream the butter and sugar until light and fluffy. Beat in the eggs one at a time. Fold in the remaining ingredients. Spread the mixture evenly in the tin. For the 2-oven Aga, put the cake on the oven shelf on the bottom set of runners of the roasting oven. Slide the cold plain shelf in two runners down from the top. For the 4-oven Aga, bake in the same position in the baking oven.

Bake for ³/₄ hour, checking occasionally that the cake is not browning too much. If it is, cover with a layer of foil. The cake is baked when it has shrunk from the sides of the tin and a skewer comes out cleanly.

Cool in the tin for 30 minutes before turning out. This cake can be made in the Aga cake baker: bake for 1 hour and test in the usual way.

# JACKY'S SULTANA AND CHERRY CAKE

.......................................................

This is quite a rich fruit cake, and the moist fruit gives it bags of flavour. The recipe came from my friend Jacky, and has become a firm favourite, especially with the men!

*1 lb/450g sultanas*
*12 oz/350g glacé cherries*
*8 oz/225g plain flour*
*pinch salt*
*6 oz/175g butter – softened*
*grated rind ¹/₂ lemon*
*6 oz/175g caster sugar*
*4 eggs*

Grease and line an 8-inch/20-cm deep cake tin. For the 2-oven Aga, heat the empty outer container of the cake baker in the roasting oven. Cut the cherries in half, wash and dry them. Mix with the sultanas and 2 tablespoons of the flour.

Soften the butter with the lemon rind and cream with the caster sugar until light and fluffy. Whisk the eggs and gradually beat into the butter mixture, adding a little flour with each addition of egg.

Stir in the remaining flour and the prepared fruit. Put mixture in the cake tin and level the surface.

For the 2-oven Aga, place the tin in the pre-heated cake baker and bake for approximately 1¹/₂ hours until risen, golden and a skewer inserted in the middle comes out clean. Cool. For the 4-oven Aga, bake the cake with the oven shelf on the floor of the baking oven for 2 hours. If after one hour, it is sufficiently brown, cover with foil. Test as before. Cool.

# SWISS ROLL

...................................................

This is my quick standby cake. It is very quick to prepare, the filling of jam is rolled in when hot. If you have only eaten shop-bought Swiss roll you have a surprise in store, because this will be light and moist. For a summer special, unroll the cake when cold and fill with whipped cream and chopped strawberries.

*3 oz/75g caster sugar*
*3 eggs*
*3 oz/75g self-raising flour*
*3 tbsp raspberry jam*
*a little extra caster sugar*

Grease and line a 12 inch x 9 inch (30cm x 22cm) Swiss roll tin. Sieve the flour onto a plate. Place the eggs and sugar in a bowl and whisk, using an electric whisk, until thick and foamy, thick enough to leave a trail.

Sieve the flour and fold it into the mixture with a tablespoon, using a cut-and-fold motion. Take care not to knock out the air, so that you keep a light, fluffy mixture. Pour the mixture into the Swiss roll tin. Allow to level off in the tin. Place the oven shelf on the floor of the roasting oven. Put in the Swiss roll and bake for 8 minutes until evenly brown and springy to the touch.

While the cake is in the oven, put the jam to warm on top of the Aga – this makes spreading easier. Lay a sheet of greaseproof paper – slightly larger than the cake tin – on the work surface and sprinkle with caster sugar.

When baked, remove the cake from the oven and immediately tip out onto the sugared greaseproof paper. Peel off the lining paper carefully. Spread the jam evenly over the cake – take care, this is a very light cake! Starting with the shortest end nearest you roll the cake fairly tightly into a roll. Allow to cool and set with the join at the bottom.

### CHOCOLATE SWISS ROLL
*Use: 2 oz/50g self-raising flour and 1 oz/25g cocoa powder – sieved together and used as flour.*

Continue as before, omitting the jam stage. Roll up the sugared paper and the Swiss roll and allow the cake to set and cool. When cold, unroll it carefully and fill with either buttercream or whipped cream. Re-roll and dust with icing or caster sugar.

..............

# CHOCOLATE SWIRLY TRAYBAKE

........................................................

Traybakes are so useful when cooking for a crowd, or to give to coffee mornings, fêtes and so on. This recipe gives the basic quantities needed for the small roasting tin; double them for the large roasting tin. For a range of flavourings that can be used, see the variations at the end of the recipe.

*3 eggs*
*6 oz/175g caster sugar*
*6 oz/175g soft margarine*
*8 oz/225g self-raising flour*
*2 tbsp boiling water and 1 tbsp cocoa powder – blended together*

Line the small roasting tin with foil. The easiest way is to turn the tin upside down and mould a sheet of foil over it. Remove the foil gently, invert the tin and carefully put the shaped foil into the tin. Grease lightly.

Put the eggs, sugar, margarine and flour into a bowl and beat them to make a light, even mixture.

Using up about half the mixture, put spoonfuls of mixture in the prepared tin.

Add the cocoa paste to the remaining cake mixture and beat gently to blend. Fill in the spaces in the cake tin with the chocolate mixture. Even the top and give one swirl to the cake with a knife.

To bake, slide the tin onto the lowest set of runners of the roasting oven for the 2-oven Aga and the baking oven for the 4-oven Aga. For the 2-oven Aga, slide in the cold sheet on the second set of runners from the top. Bake for 25 minutes until risen, evenly golden and slightly shrunk from the sides of the tin. Remove from the tin and cool. Dust with icing sugar or ice with chocolate fudge icing.

## CHOCOLATE FUDGE ICING

*2 oz/50g margarine*
*2 oz/50g cocoa – sieved*
*1 lb/450g icing sugar – sieved*
*about 3 tbsp milk*

Melt the margarine in a saucepan, add cocoa and stir over a gentle heat for 1 minute. Remove from heat. Stir in icing sugar and as much milk as needed to make a smooth, spreading consistency.

Pour over the cake and spread evenly. Allow to set before cutting the cake into squares.

**VARIATIONS:**
• *using the basic cake mix without the cocoa*
• *fruit: 6 oz/175g dried fruit*
• *cherry: 4 oz/100g chopped glacé cherries*

# VICTORIA SANDWICH

Sponge cakes baked in the Aga are spongey and moist. Do not let anyone tell you a cake cannot be made in an Aga, just try this simple all-in-one method. I have given ideas for variations on flavours – you may want to try your own ideas. For puddings, try topping cooked fruit or jam with the sponge mixture and baking in the same way. Small cakes can be made with the same mixture – fill lined bun tins and bake for 15-20 minutes. Ice the tops to make cup cakes or fairy cakes.

*3 eggs*
*6 oz/175g self-raising flour*
*6 oz/175g caster sugar*
*6 oz/175g soft margarine*
*raspberry jam to sandwich*
*caster sugar for top*

Grease and base-line two 8-inch/20-cm Victoria sandwich tins. Measure the eggs, flour, sugar and butter into a bowl and beat with a wooden spoon or an electric mixer until light and fluffy – do not overbeat. Divide the mixture between the tins and level the top. Place the tins on the oven shelf on the floor of the 2-oven model. Slide the cold shelf two runners above the top of the tins. Bake for 25-30 minutes until golden brown and springy to the touch. With the oven shelf on the floor of the baking oven of the 4-oven model, bake for 25-30 minutes until golden brown and springy to the touch. Turn out onto a cooling rack. When cool, sandwich together with jam and dust the top with caster sugar.

### VARIATIONS

LEMON:add the grated rind of 1 lemon to the cake mixture. Sandwich together with lemon curd and cream. Dust with sugar.

CHOCOLATE: mix 1 tablespoon of cocoa powder with 2 tablespoons of hot water and 1 teaspoon of treacle. Add to cake mix. Sandwich together with 4 oz/100g Greek-style yoghurt and 4 oz/100g melted chocolate beaten together. Sprinkle the top with grated chocolate.

COFFEE AND WALNUT: mix 2 teaspoons of instant coffee granules with 1 tablespoon of hot water. Add to cake mixture with 2 oz/50g finely chopped walnuts. Sandwich together with coffee butter icing – 8 oz/225g sieved icing sugar, 4 oz/100g soft margarine and 2 teaspoons of the coffee mixed with 1 tablespoon of hot water, beaten well together. Spread the remaining icing on top and decorate with walnut halves.

# PASSION CAKE

I am not sure why this bears the name "Passion Cake", maybe because it is moist and luscious and we become passionate for the cake – or the cook! This is a truly tasty carrot cake, the best I have ever tried.

*10 oz/275g plain flour*
*1 level tsp salt*
*1 level tsp bicarbonate of soda*
*2 level tsp baking powder*
*6 oz/175g soft brown sugar*
*3 eggs*
*2 ripe bananas*
*6 oz/175g grated carrots*
*2 oz/50g finely chopped walnuts*
*6 fl oz/175g light corn oil*

FROSTING
*3 oz/75g butter*
*3 oz/75g cream cheese*
*6 oz/175g icing sugar*
*1/2 tsp vanilla essence*
*walnuts to decorate*

Sift flour, salt, bicarbonate of soda and baking powder into a mixing bowl. Add the sugar and chopped nuts. Crack in the eggs, add mashed bananas and grated carrot. Add the corn oil and beat the mixture well to make a soft cake batter.

Divide between two greased and lined 8-inch/20-cm sandwich tins. Have the oven shelf on the floor of the oven. For the 2-oven Aga, slide the cold shelf onto the second set of runners down. For the 4-oven Aga, use the baking oven. Bake the cakes for 30 minutes, until risen and firm to the touch. Turn onto a cooling rack and cool.

### FROSTING

Beat the butter and cheese together until soft. Beat in the sieved icing sugar and vanilla essence to make a soft and creamy frosting. Use about one third of the frosting to sandwich the cakes together. Spread the remainder on the top. Decorate with either whole or chopped walnuts.

# BOSTON CREAM PIE

This is a slight variation on a Victoria sandwich that I remember my mother making for special occasions. The cream filling is also useful for filling fruit tarts and meringues.

*6 oz/175g butter*
*6 oz/175g caster sugar*
*4 eggs*
*8 oz/225g self-raising flour*

### CREAM FILLING
*2 egg yolks*
*2¹/₂ oz/65g castor sugar*
*a few drops of vanilla essence*
*³/₄ oz/20g flour*
*good ¹/₄ pint/150ml milk*

### CHOCOLATE ICING
*1 oz/25g plain chocolate*
*2 oz/50g icing sugar – sieved*
*1¹/₂ tbsp water*

Grease and base-line two sandwich cake tins. Cream the butter and sugar, beat in the eggs and fold in the flour. Add 1 tablespoon of warm water, if needed, to make a soft dropping consistency. Divide between tins.

Place the oven shelf on the floor of the roasting oven. Put in the cake tins and slide the cold shelf two runners above the top of the tins. For the 4-oven Aga, put on the shelf on the bottom set of runners in the baking oven. Bake for 25-35 minutes until risen, golden and slightly shrunk from the sides of the tin. Turn on to a cooling rack – cool.

For the filling, cream the egg yolks and sugar until light and fluffy. Mix in the flour and milk. Cook over gentle heat, stirring until thickened. Stir in the vanilla essence. Set aside to cool.

Melt the chocolate in a basin on the top of the Aga. Stir into icing sugar with the water. Beat well until smooth. Sandwich the cakes with the filling and pour over the chocolate icing. Leave until the icing is set.

# RICH STICKY GINGERBREAD

A delicious sticky, moist gingerbread. It is good to eat on the day of making, but even nicer a day or two later. Store in an airtight tin

*12 oz/350g plain flour*
*2 level tsp ground ginger*
*2 level tsp ground cinnamon*
*8 oz/225g butter*
*8 oz/225g soft brown sugar*
*4 oz/100g golden syrup*
*4 oz/100g black treacle*
*1/2 pint/300ml milk*
*2 level tsp bicarbonate of soda*
*2 eggs*

Line the small roasting tin with foil and lightly grease it. Sieve together the flour and spices. Stand the milk in a measuring jug on top of the Aga to warm.

Melt the sugar, syrup, treacle and butter in a large saucepan. Stir well over a

gentle heat. Remove from the heat and stir in the flour and spices. Add the bicarbonate of soda to the warm milk. Stir the milk into the syrup mixture and beat well with a wooden spoon. Beat the eggs together in a basin. Stir into the gingerbread mixture.

Pour into the prepared tin. For a 2-oven Aga, hang in the roasting oven, on the bottom set of runners. Slide in the cold shelf, two runners above. Bake for 30-40 minutes until risen, firm to the touch and slightly shrunken from the sides of the tin. For the 4-oven Aga, bake in the baking oven on the bottom set of runners for 30-40 minutes, turn round half way through cooking. Cool in the tin.

**Cut into 20 portions.**

# CHOCOLATE ECLAIRS

Eclairs are actually very easy to make and fairly quick too. To make profiteroles for a pudding make the éclairs into rounds using a spoon.

### CHOUX PASTRY
*2¹/₂ oz/65g plain flour*
*pinch salt*
*¹/₄ pint/150ml water*
*2 oz/50g butter – cubed*
*2 eggs – well beaten*

*¹/₂ pint/300ml double cream, for the filling*

### CHOCOLATE GLACE ICING
*3 oz/75g plain chocolate*
*1 oz/25g butter*
*3 tbsp warm water*
*¹/₂ tsp vanilla essence*
*6 oz/175g icing sugar*

Sieve the flour and salt. Put water and butter into a saucepan, stand on the simmering plate and heat to melt the butter. Then bring to a brisk boil. Remove from the heat, quickly tip in all the flour and beat well with a wooden spoon. Return to the heat and stir briskly until the dough forms a ball and the sides of the pan are left clean. Remove from heat.

Add the eggs gradually, beating between each addition. I find a hand-held electric mixer best. Beat until a smooth, shiny mixture is formed.

Fit a piping bag with ½ -inch/1-cm plain nozzle and fill it with the pastry. Pipe lengths 4 inch/10cm long on to a greased baking tray. This makes about 1 dozen.

For the 2- and 4-oven Agas, have the shelf on the lowest set of runners of the roasting oven and bake for 20-25 minutes until risen and golden brown. Remove from the oven and slit the sides to allow steam to escape. Return to the oven for 5 minutes to dry out. Cool on a wire rack.

Whip cream and fill the éclairs. Cover the tops with the icing and leave to set.

### CHOCOLATE GLACE ICING

Break chocolate into a basin, add the butter and stand the basin on top of the Aga to melt. When melted add the water and vanilla essence. Gradually add the icing sugar, beating until smooth. Coat the éclairs. For a pudding, fill the éclairs with cream, pile high on a dish and pour the chocolate icing over them.

### VARIATION: COFFEE GLACE ICING

*8 oz/225g icing sugar*
*2 tbsp hot water*
*2 tsp instant coffee granules*

Mix the coffee granules and hot water until dissolved. Sieve the sugar in a bowl, gradually add the coffee and beat well until the icing is thick enough to coat the back of a wooden spoon.

# SHORTBREAD

This is a traditional Scottish shortbread, but I have suggested some variations to ring the changes. This shortbread, packed in a pretty box or basket, makes a lovely gift. Always use butter for flavour and a crisp texture.

*6 oz/175g plain flour*
*4 oz/100g butter*
*2 oz/50g caster sugar*

Cut the butter into small cubes and add to the flour. Rub in well, then add the sugar. Continue to rub and work until the mixture forms a ball. Divide the

mixture in two. Roll to ¹/₄ inch/5mm thickness and 8-inch/20-cm circles. Slide each circle onto a baking tray.

For the 2-oven Aga, place the oven shelf on the floor of the oven. Slide in the baking trays. Slide the cold shelf on third set of runners down. For the 4-oven Aga, bake in the baking oven, the shelf on the floor of the oven.

Bake for 15-20 minutes until dry and a very pale golden colour. Cool on a wire rack. Dust with caster sugar.

### VARIATIONS
•Replace 1 oz/25g flour with 1 oz/25g ground rice for a slight crunch
•Use wholemeal flour
•Add 1 oz/25g finely chopped cherries
•Replace 1 oz/25g flour with 1 oz/25g ground almonds

# ETHEL'S SHORTCAKE BISCUITS

Ethel was a dear friend of my mother's. She was a cook/housekeeper who produced delicate, tasty food. We always had these crisp biscuits with fine Earl Grey tea, but they are equally nice with fruit salads – or just straight from the biscuit tin!

*4 oz/100g self-raising flour*
*2¹/₄ oz/65g butter*
*1¹/₂ oz/35g icing sugar*
*yolk of 1 egg*

Rub the butter into the flour to the consistency of fine breadcrumbs. Stir in the icing sugar. Add the egg yolk and work it in until the dough binds together. Wrap and chill for ¹/₂ hour. Roll to ¹/₄ inch 1cm thickness and stamp out circles, space out on 2 baking trays. In the 2-oven Aga, bake with the oven shelf on the floor of the roasting oven and the cold plain shelf on the second set of runners from the top. In the 4-oven Aga, bake with the oven shelf on the floor of the baking oven. Bake for 8-12 minutes until pale gold.

# CHRISTMAS BUTTER BISCUITS

.....................................................

I make batches of these and give them as little offerings when visiting friends at Christmas. My children cut out Christmas shapes to give to teachers and elderly neighbours. They are truly crisp and delicious.

*8 oz/225g butter*
*7 oz/200g caster sugar*
*2 eggs – beaten*
*1 tbsp ground almonds*
*14 oz/400g plain flour*
*1¹/₂ tsp baking powder*
*¹/₂ tsp salt*
*grated rind of 1 lemon*

Cream the butter and the sugar. Add the eggs and all remaining ingredients. Knead lightly. The dough will be slightly sticky. Wrap in cling film and chill for at least one hour. Cut into quarters. Work with one quarter while the remaining three quarters stay chilled. Roll to thickness of a 10p piece. Cut out shapes. Place on lightly greased baking trays.

For the 2-oven Aga, have the oven shelf on the bottom set of runners. Place baking trays in the oven, slide the cold plain shelf on second set of runners down. For the 4-oven Aga, bake towards the bottom of the baking oven. Bake for 7-10 minutes until slightly golden at the edges. Cool on a wire rack. These biscuits can be iced with water icing.When baking a large batch of biscuits, remove the cold plain shelf periodically and allow to cool.

# MINCE PIES

.........................................

My good friend Jane, who helps me with my Aga Cookery Days, is an excellent cook and makes the best mince pies I have ever tasted; this is her recipe .

*12 oz/350g plain white flour*
*8 oz/225g butter*
*4 oz/100g caster sugar*
*1 lb/450g jar mincemeat*
*caster sugar to dust*

Sieve the flour into a bowl and stir in the sugar. Rub in the butter until it resembles breadcrumbs. Continue to rub in until the shortbread binds together. If the mixture is soft and sticky, wrap and chill for half an hour.

Roll out and cut 12 circles – not too thinly – to line the bun tins. Re-roll the shortbread and cut out 12 tops. Stars and bells are good, festive shapes. Line the tins, spoon in 1 dessertspoonful of mincemeat – do not overfill. Top with the shaped lids. Bake directly on the floor of the roasting oven for 15-20 minutes. Remove from the oven and dust immediately with caster sugar (it will stick on better when the mince pies are hot). This quantity will make 1 dozen pies.

# GINGERBREAD SHAPES

.........................................

This makes a firm biscuit suitable for gingerbread men and other shapes, stars for Christmas, rabbits for Easter etc. Children love rolling and cutting these and, when cooked, they can be decorated with icing and dragees.

*2 tbsp golden syrup and*
*1 tbsp black treacle*
*2¹/₂ oz/65g soft brown sugar*
*1 tbsp water*
*3¹/₂ oz/90g margarine*
*1 level tsp ground cinnamon*
*1 level tsp ground ginger*
*pinch ground nutmeg*
*grated rind of ¹/₂ an orange*

*¹/₂ level tsp bicarbonate of soda*
*about 8 oz/225g plain flour*

Warm the syrup and treacle on top of the Aga before measuring. Put syrup, treacle, sugar, spices, water, margarine and orange rind into a saucepan. Bring to the boil on the simmering plate, stirring all the time.

Remove from heat and stir in bicarbonate of soda. Gradually stir in flour, beating well between each addition and making sure there are no lumps. Add as much flour as is needed to make a stiff dough. Chill the mixture, wrapped, for at least 30 minutes. The dough will now be firm enough to roll out. Roll on a floured worktop until the thickness of two 20p pieces. Stamp out shapes and place them on greased baking trays. Continue rolling and stamping out to use up all the dough. Remember to put holes in the shapes if the finished biscuits are to be hung up.

Bake in the roasting oven with the oven shelf on the bottom set of runners and the cold shelf two runners above. For a 4-oven Aga, bake in the baking oven, on the bottom set of runners. Bake until dry-looking, about 10 minutes. Allow to set on the baking tray for a minute or two before removing to a wire rack.

# DEMERARA CRUNCH BISCUITS

*10 oz/275g self-raising flour*
*8 oz/225g soft margarine*
*5 oz/150g demerara sugar*
*2 tsp ground ginger*

Mix all the ingredients together to give a stiffish dough. Roll small walnut-sized pieces into balls, and space them well apart on greased baking trays. Using a fork dipped in water, press each biscuit down gently. With the oven shelf on the bottom set of runners in the roasting oven, slide the biscuits in. Put the cold shelf on the top set of runners. for the 4-oven Aga, put the oven shelf on the middle set of runners in the baking oven. Bake for 10-12 minutes until a light golden colour. Cool on a wire rack.

# CHOCOLATE CHIP COOKIES

......................................

This is the best recipe for a crunchy biscuit with chunks of chocolate. Make giant cookies, one or two to a tray, for parties as going-home presents, or just to fill the biscuit tin.

*8 oz/225g soft margarine*
*6 oz/175g soft brown sugar*
*4 oz/100g caster sugar*
*1 tsp vanilla essence*
*2 eggs – beaten*
*11 oz/300g self-raising flour*
*8 oz/225g chocolate chips*

Cream the margarine and sugars together. Beat in the eggs and vanilla essence, fold in the flour and chocolate chips. Place spoonfuls on the greased baking trays, allowing room to spread.

For a 2-oven Aga, place oven shelf on bottom set of runners in the roasting oven. Slide in biscuits. Place cold plain shelf on second set of runners down. For the 4-oven Aga, bake on the middle set of runners in the baking oven. Bake for 10-15 minutes until lightly browned. Allow to set slightly on baking tray before removing to a cooling rack

# CINNAMON BUTTER COOKIES

......................................

These are unusual chunky biscuits, ideal on their own or with fruit salad.

*4 oz/100g butter*
*2 oz/50g caster sugar*
*3 oz/75g plain flour*
*2 oz/50g semolina*
*1 tbsp ground cinnamon*
*1 oz/25g dessicated coconut*

Cream butter and sugar until light and fluffy. Sieve together the flour, cinnamon and semolina. Work the dry ingredients plus coconut into creamed mixture. Knead lightly to give a manageable dough.

Place dough in the centre of a greased baking tray. Pat out to a 7-inch/18-cm square. Neaten edges, prick with a fork. Bake with the oven shelf on the floor of the roasting oven of the 2-oven Aga, with the cold shelf 2 runners above the tray. Put the oven shelf on the floor of the baking oven of the 4-oven Aga.

Bake for 25-30 minutes until pale golden and looking dry. Cut into portions and cool on a wire rack.

# SCONES

A lot of people tell me they cannot make scones. There are rules to follow: have the dough moist, a cross between a cake mix and pastry; do not take a rolling pin to scone dough, press lightly with your hand to just the thickness of your hand; bake in a hot oven.

*8 oz/225g self-raising flour*
*1 oz/25g butter*
*pinch salt*
*¹/₄ – ¹/₂ pint/150-300ml milk*
*one flavouring ingredient*

FLAVOURINGS:
*1 oz/25g sugar*
*2 oz/50g grated cheese*
*¹/₂ oz/15g sultanas*

Sieve flour and salt. Rub in the butter. Stir in ¹/₄ pint/150ml milk, using a knife, to make a soft but not sticky dough. Use extra milk if needed. Add the flavouring of your choice. Turn the dough onto a floured worksurface – treat LIGHTLY!

Press down with the palm of the hand until the thickness of the hand. Stamp out shapes with a cutter. Place on a baking tray and brush the tops with a little milk. In the roasting oven place the shelf on the third set of runners from the top. Bake the scones for 10-15 minutes until well risen, golden brown and firm to the touch. Serve warm with butter. Cool the scones if serving with jam and cream.

# A M E R I C A N   M U F F I N S

.................................................

This is a truly American recipe. Another quick cake for hungry hoards! Vary the flavourings according to what is in the store cupboard. They are good for breakfast made with wholemeal flour and served with butter and honey. Use traditional deep muffin tins or smaller English bun tins. I have used tea-cup measures — accuracy is not important.

*1¹/₂ cups plain flour*
*¹/₂ cup sugar*
*¹/₂ tsp salt*
*2 tsp baking powder*
*1 egg*
*¹/₂ cup milk*
*¹/₄ cup vegetable oil*
*one flavouring ingredient*

### F L A V O U R I N G S
*1 cup chopped apple and ¹/₂ tsp cinnamon*
*1 oz/25g chocolate chips*
*¹/₄ cup raisins*
*¹/₂ carton blueberry yoghurt*

Sieve together the flour, sugar, salt and baking powder. Stir in the flavouring of your choice. Beat the egg, add milk and oil. Stir into dry ingredients until evenly moistened.

Fill muffin tins lined with cake cases. Bake on second set of runners from top of the roasting oven. Bake for 15-20 minutes until risen and browned. Serve warm with butter.

**Makes approximately ¹/₂ dozen muffins.**

.................................................

# MERINGUES

...................................................

This is the best way I know to use up egg whites. This method gives a very dry, crisp meringue that can be stored for several weeks, very useful if preparing for a party. When cold, store in an airtight tin or wrap in a clean tea-towel, in a basket in the airing cupboard. This is a good, dry storage place provided you do not hang damp clothes to dry in there! Because these are crisp meringues they can be filled an hour ot two in advance and will not go too soft.

*2 egg whites*
*4 oz/100g caster sugar*
*¹/₂ tsp cornflour*
*¹/₂ tsp white wine vinegar*
*¹/₄ pint/150ml double cream, for the filling – whipped to soft peaks*

In a clean, grease-free bowl whisk egg whites until white and fluffy. Add the sugar, 1 teaspoonful at a time, whisking well after each addition.

Blend the cornflour and vinegar together, whisk in after all the sugar. The meringue mixture should be thick and fluffy.

Line a baking tray with baking parchment – not greaseproof paper. Using a dessertspoon, spoon out individual meringues onto the prepared tray.

Put the oven shelf on the bottom set of runners of the simmering oven. Slide in the meringues. Dry out for 2 hours. Leave them overnight. My simmering oven is quite warm, so I leave the door slightly ajar all night. This will give crisp, white meringues.

Sandwich with whipped cream up to one hour before serving.

### VARIATION:
*use 2 oz/50g caster sugar and 2 oz/50g soft brown sugar instead of all caster sugar, for a caramel flavour*

# SCOTCH PANCAKES

......................................................

These are every Aga-owner's standby. They are quick and easy to make when there are hungry mouths to feed and nothing in the cake tin. Guests, who always lean against the Aga rail, can often be persuaded to cook a batch of pancakes whilst you get on with the table-laying. Children love to make their own pancakes, especially in the shape of their initials. These can be sweet or savoury. I like them plain with crispy bacon!

*4 oz/100g self-raising flour*
*pinch salt*
*1 egg*
*¹/₄ pint/150ml milk*

Measure the flour and salt into a bowl. Make a well in the centre, add the egg and half the milk and beat well, then stir in the remaining milk to make a thick batter. Brush and then lightly grease the simmering plate. Spoon the batter onto the simmering plate, spacing well apart, about 6 or 7 at a time.

When bubbles rise to the surface, turn the pancakes over, using a fish slice. Cook for about a minute on the second side until golden brown. Lift off and keep warm on a plate in the simmering oven whilst all the batter is being used up. Serve warm with butter. If you are making a large batch it may be necessary to put the lid down for a few minutes to warm up the simmering plate.

### OPTIONAL FLAVOURINGS
*1 oz/25g caster sugar*
*grated rind of ¹/₂ a lemon*
*1 oz/25g sultanas*
*2 oz/50g wholemeal flour and 2 oz/50g white flour*
*2 oz/50g buckwheat flour and 2 oz/50g white flour*

# WELSH CAKES

......................................................

These are quick and easy to make and taste delicious straight from the simmering plate with lots of real butter.

*2 oz/50g butter*
*2 oz/50g lard*
*8 oz/225g self-raising flour*
*2 oz/50g caster sugar*
*$1/2$ tsp grated nutmeg*
*3 oz/75g currants*
*1 egg*
*milk to mix*

Rub the fats into the flour, stir in the sugar, spice and currants. Make a soft but manageable dough with the beaten egg – and some milk if necessary. Divide the dough in half. Pat out on a floured worktop into two rounds approximately the thickness of the hand. Cut into 8 triangles per round.

Brush the surface of the simmering plate and oil lightly. Cook the Welsh cakes spread out on the plate, 4-5 minutes on each side to cook through. They may darken, but they are still delicious. If they cook too fast on the outside or if you know the simmering plate is very hot, leave the lid up for a few minutes before starting to cook.

Serve warm, straight from the hot plate, split and buttered.

**Makes 16.**
......................................................

# YEAST COOKERY

## QUICK BREAD

If you want to make bread, but are short on time, use this method. It is even quicker with a large capacity food processor.

*1¹/₂ lb/675g strong white flour and/or wholemeal flour*
*2 tsp salt*
*1 sachet easy blend yeast*
*1 tbsp cooking oil*
*³/₄ pint/450ml warm water*

Measure flour, salt and yeast into a mixing bowl and stir. Add the oil and the warm water – it must not be hot. Add ¹/₂ pint/300ml to start with and mix in to make a pliable dough. Add more water as necessary. Transfer to a floured worktop and knead for 5 minutes until smooth and stretchy.

Shape the dough into rolls or loaves. This quantity will make two small loaves or about 16 rolls. Place in well greased tins and cover with a clean cloth. Stand on a cloth on the lid of the simmering plate until doubled in size. Glaze with beaten egg. Bake in the roasting oven – loaves on the bottom set of runners for 30 minutes, rolls on the third set of runners for 15-20 minutes.

To test if cooked, tap the bottom: if the bread sounds hollow it is baked. Cool on a wire rack.

# FARMER'S BREAD

This recipe makes a moist, chewy loaf, rather different to traditional English bread. It is delicious with cheese and pickles or slices of ham. This recipe makes 1 large loaf.

*14 oz/400g plain strong white flour*
*5 oz/150g wholemeal flour*
*5 oz/150g rye flour*
*1 tbsp salt*
*1 oz/25g fresh yeast or 1 sachet easy blend yeast*
*8 fl oz/225ml warm water*
*7 fl oz/200ml buttermilk or plain yoghurt*

Mix together the flours and the salt. Crumble in the fresh yeast, or sprinkle in the easy blend yeast. Add the warm water and the buttermilk or yoghurt. Knead well by hand or with the dough blade in a processor to form a fairly firm dough which leaves the bowl clean.

Stand the bowl on top of a folded tea-towel on the simmering plate lid, cover the bowl with a tea-towel and allow to rise until doubled in size, about half an hour. Knock back the dough and form it into a ball. Drape the tea-towel into a bowl or basket and flour it well. Put in the dough and put to rise again until doubled in size, about 30 minutes.

Invert the loaf carefully onto a greased and floured baking tray. Make a lattice of cuts onto the loaf's surface. Slide the tray into the roasting oven, with the oven shelf on the third set of runners from the top. Bake for 35–45 minutes until golden, crusty and sounding hollow on the bottom when tapped. Cool on a wire rack.

# PLAITED MILK LOAF

This is a rich bread that looks attractive on the bread board. It goes particularly well with home-made jam and good butter. Plaiting is not difficult and the bread rises after shaping to give a very attractive appearance.

*1¹/₂ lb/675g strong, white flour*
*2 tsp salt*
*1 oz/25g fresh yeast or 1 sachet easy-blend yeast*
*3 oz/75g soft butter*
*about 15 fl oz/450ml milk*
*1 egg, beaten, to glaze*

Measure the milk into a jug and stand on the Aga top to warm. Combine the flour, salt and sachet yeast (if using) in a bowl. Rub in the butter.

If using fresh yeast blend this with half the warm milk. Add to the flour mixture, mixing in more milk, if needed, to make a smooth and springy dough which comes cleanly from the bowl. Knead well on a floured surface for 10 minutes, or 5 minutes in a food processor, until the dough is stretchy.

Put the dough to rise in a bowl, stand on a folded tea-towel on top of the simmering plate lid. Cover with a clean cloth until doubled in size, about 30 minutes. Alternatively, loosely cover with cling film and put in the fridge overnight.

Knock back the dough and cut in half. Roll out 2 long sausage shapes. Place on a floured surface, putting one shape over the other to form an even cross. Cross over the bottom sausage of dough – retaining the cross appearance. Continue using alternate sides. When complete put the dough on its side – you will see a plait shape – and tuck in the loose ends.

Lay onto a well greased and floured baking tray and leave to rise on top of the simmering plate for about 15 minutes until risen and puffy.

Brush well with beaten egg. Have the oven shelf on the third set of runners from the top in the roasting oven. Put in the tray of bread and bake for about 40-45 minutes until golden brown and sounding hollow when tapped on the bottom. Cool on a wire rack.

# FOCCACIA

An increasingly popular Italian flat bread, foccacia is delicious with summer salads and good for mopping up excess French dressing. My recipe uses fresh rosemary, which has a strong flavour, leave out the rosemary if you want a plainer bread.

*1 lb/450g strong white flour*
*1 tsp salt*
*1 oz/25g fresh yeast or 1 sachet easy-blend yeast*
*4 tbsp good olive oil*
*about 8 fl oz/225ml warm water*
*olive oil,*
*coarse sea salt*
*fresh rosemary leaves*

Mix the flour and the salt in a bowl. Add the dried yeast to the flour or blend the fresh yeast with a little warm water. Stir in the olive oil and most of the water, adding more water if necessary to make a manageable dough. Turn onto a floured worktop and knead for about 5 minutes until smooth and pliable. Return to the mixing bowl and cover with a tea towel. Stand on a folded tea-towel on top of the simmering plate lid. Allow to rise until doubled in size – about 30 minutes.

Knock back the dough, roll out to an oblong about $^3/_4$ inch/2cm thick and about 12 inch x 8 inch/30x20cm in size. Place on a well greased and floured baking tray. Return to the top of the Aga to rise. Using the end of a wooden spoon handle, make deep indentations over the surface of the dough. Drizzle over about 2 tablespoons of olive oil, scatter with sea salt and the rosemary leaves.

Bake in the roasting oven, with the shelf on the third set of runners from the top for about 20-30 minutes until risen and golden brown. Cool on a wire rack.

# FLAVOURED BREADS

The range of breads available today can be mind boggling. I love to see what is new in the shops, but I do draw breath at the cost of some of the more exotic or interesting breads. They are easy to make, cost a fraction of the commercial variety and very often taste better. I like to make a mixed variety of breads, sometimes loaves or sometimes a ring of rolls taken from the variety made. Grease a 9inch/23-cm round cake tin, shape 8 rolls, place 7 round the outside of the tin and one in the middle. Rise and bake in the usual way. This quantity will make two small loaves. The quantity of flavourings given is enough for one loaf.

*1¹/₂ lb/675g strong white flour*
*1 tbsp salt*
*2 tbsp olive oil*
*1 oz/25g fresh yeast or 1 sachet easy-blend yeast*
*about 12 fl oz/350ml warm water*
*1 egg, to glaze*

Put the flour, salt and oil in a large bowl. Add the easy-blend yeast, or blend fresh yeast with half the water. Add to the flour mixture. Stir well, adding more water to make a smooth pliable dough. If making by hand, transfer to a floured worktop and knead for 5-10 minutes until smooth and pliable. If using a machine, 4-5 minutes kneading is sufficient. Cover with a cloth, stand on top of a folded tea-towel placed on top of the simmering plate lid. Leave to rise until doubled in size – about 30 minutes.

On a floured worktop, divide the dough in half, knead in the chosen flavourings for each loaf. Grease and flour two 1lb/450g loaf tins or large baking trays. Shape the loaves and put them in the tins. Put to rise again on the simmering plate lid until doubled in size – again about 30 minutes. Brush the tops with beaten egg. To bake, have the oven shelf on the third or fourth set of runners from the top of the roasting oven, to allow some rising – this will depend upon the type of tin used. Bake for 30 minutes, remove from the tins – or turn upside down if using a baking tray – return to the oven for 10 minutes until the bread is crisp and sounds hollow when knocked. Cool on wire rack.

## FLAVOURINGS

*3 oz/75g stoned olives*
*4 tbsp freshly chopped mixed herbs*
*2 tbsp chopped sun-dried tomatoes (the olive oil in the recipe can be replaced with the tomato oil)*
*3 oz/75g freshly grated Gruyère or Sbrinz*
*3 oz/75g finely chopped walnuts*

# GARLIC BREAD

........................................................

*1 French stick*
*4-6 oz/100-175g butter, softened – depending upon the size of loaf*
*2-3 cloves garlic*

Mash the butter in a bowl until softened. Beat in the peeled and crushed cloves of garlic. Cut the French stick into slices about 1½ inch/4 cm wide, but do not cut right through. Spread the butter between the cuts.

Spread a little butter over the top. Wrap the loaf in foil and heat through in the roasting oven, have the shelf on the third set of runners from the top, for about 10-15 minutes until piping hot and the butter has melted.

**OTHER BUTTER FLAVOURS:**
*2 tbsp of chopped mixed herbs*
*2 tbsp chopped parsley*
*2 cloves of garlic and 1 tbsp mixed chopped herbs*
*3 tbsp lemon juice*

# BATH BUNS

Bath is my adopted city and the most attractive place to live. One traditional food that visitors to Bath always enjoy is a Bath bun. Split and serve with good butter when freshly made.

*1½ lb/675g strong white flour*
*1 oz/25g fresh yeast*
*½ tsp salt*
*1 tsp sugar*
*8 fl oz/225ml warm milk*
*3 oz/75g butter – melted*
*4 eggs*
*4 oz/100g caster sugar*
*½ oz/15g cut mixed peel*
*2 oz/50g currants*

............

*beaten egg to glaze*
*2 tbsp milk and 1 tbsp sugar boiled together for a sticky glaze*
*2 tbsp granulated sugar*

Blend the yeast and 1 teaspoon of the sugar together until runny. Mix in 2 tablespoons of the warm milk. Leave for a few minutes on the Aga until frothy. Measure the flour, sugar and salt into a mixing bowl. In a well in the middle add the beaten eggs, the melted butter and the yeast mixture with the rest of the milk. Mix all together to make a soft, manageable dough. Do this by hand, with a mixer and dough hook or in a large processor. Put the dough on a floured work surface and knead until smooth, adding more flour if the dough should be sticky.

Return to a clean bowl, cover with a tea-towel and stand on a trivet or folded tea-towel on top of the simmering plate lid. Leave until the dough has doubled in size. Remove from the bowl onto a floured work surface, knock back and work in the mixed peel and the currants. Cut the dough in half, shape into 2 rounds and cut each round into 8 even pieces. Shape each piece into a bun and place on a greased baking tray. Return the tray to the top of the Aga on a cloth or trivet and allow the buns to rise until doubled in size.

Brush with the beaten egg. Put one oven shelf on the third set of runners from the top of the roasting oven and the second oven shelf on the floor. Put in the 2 trays of buns and bake for 15-20 minutes, until risen, golden brown and sounding hollow when tapped. Immediately on removing from the oven brush with the sticky glaze and sprinkle over the granulated sugar. Cool on a wire rack.

**Makes 16.**

# JAMS AND PRESERVES

# STRAWBERRY JAM

...............................................

This method of making strawberry jam is quick and easy. It also gives a fresh bright colour and taste.

*7 lb/3kg strawberries*
*juice of 2 lemons*
*6 lb/2.5kg sugar*

Hull the strawberries and discard any soft or mouldy fruit. Put in a large, non-metallic bowl with the lemon juice. Add the sugar, stir gently, cover and leave to stand overnight.

The next day, transfer to a preserving pan and heat on the simmering plate to dissolve the sugar. Stir gently to avoid breaking the fruit. Transfer to the boiling plate and boil rapidly for 10-15 minutes until a teaspoonful of the mixture wrinkles after setting for 1 minute on a cool saucer. Cool the jam for a few minutes – this prevents the fruit floating to the top of the jar – before putting into warmed, sterilised jam jars. Cover and seal in the usual way.

**Makes about 10 lb/5kg.**
...............................................

# RASPBERRY PRESERVE

Raspberries are probably my favourite fruit. Eating them today brings back memories of picking pounds of them on summer evenings. My father grew enough for us to eat and to make into a wonderful, fresh-tasting jam. This method of preserving raspberries keeps their fresh flavour and is lovely in the depths of winter with fresh scones for tea. This recipe does not make a firm-set jam, but a soft, bright preserve.

*4 lb/1.8kg raspberries*
*5 lb/2.25kg sugar*

Rinse and pick over the raspberries. Spread out in a large roasting tin. Measure the sugar and spread out in a second roasting tin or two smaller tins. Place the sugar and raspberries in the roasting oven and heat for 30-40 minutes, occasionally stirring. Heat until the raspberries are soft and can be broken down. The sugar should be hot.

Remove from the oven and combine the sugar and raspberries. Stir well until the sugar has dissolved. Ladle into warm, sterilised jars. Cover and label in the usual way.

**Makes about 8 lb/3.5kg.**

# G O O S E B E R R Y   J A M

This is a lovely sweet, tangy jam. It is very easy to make because it sets so easily. Ripe, red dessert gooseberries will give quite a pink jam, the more usual green gooseberries will give a more yellow jam.

*4 lb/1.8 kg gooseberries – topped, tailed and washed*
*1 pint/600ml water*
*4 lb/1.8 kg granulated sugar*
*small knob of butter*

Put the gooseberries and the water in a large preserving pan. Place on the simmering plate and bring to the boil. Cover and place in the simmering oven for about 30 minutes, until the fruit is cooked. Remove from the oven, mash the fruit a little. Stir in the sugar and the butter.

Return to the simmering plate and stir well until the sugar has dissolved. Move to the boiling plate, bring to the boil and boil vigorously for 10 minutes. Remove from the heat and test for setting. Pour into warm sterilised jars and finish in the usual way.

**Makes about 8 lb/3.5kg.**

# KIWI PRESERVE

........................................................

When my stocks of jam are running low and there is little fruit about, I make this jam as kiwis are often on offer in supermarkets.

*1¹/₂ lb/750g Kiwi fruit*
*¹/₂ pint/250ml water*
*2 tbsp lemon juice*
*1 lb/500g granulated sugar*

Peel and finely chop the kiwi fruit. Place in a heavy based pan with the water and lemon juice. Bring to the boil, cover and place in the simmering oven for half an hour to soften the fruit.

Return the pan to the simmering plate, remove the lid and simmer to reduce the fruit to a pulp. Add the sugar and stir until dissolved. Bring to the boil and boil rapidly, probably on the boiling plate, without stirring for 15 minutes. Watch carefully, you need a good boil, but it must not boil over. Remove from the heat and test for a set, when a teaspoon of the mixture wrinkles after setting for 1 minute on a cool saucer. Remove any scum and pour into warmed, sterilised jars. Cover with a wax disc, cool and then cover with a lid and label.

**Makes 2 lb/1kg.**
........................................................

# MARMALADE

..........................................................

Homemade marmalade has a tang that commercial marmalade never matches. Even if you do not eat much yourself, it always makes welcome gifts and contributions to charity stalls. Seville oranges are available in January and February, so I find that if I am too busy at that time of year I freeze some oranges until I have some time. I do not find extra pectin is needed as mentioned in some books. This recipe is for a Seville orange marmalade, but the same method and quantities can be used for lemons and grapefruit, just make up to 3 lb/1.35kg fruit. For a dark marmalade add 1 oz/25g dark treacle with the sugar.

*3 lb/1.5kg Seville oranges*
*juice 2 lemons*
*4 pints/2.5 litres water*
*6 lb/2.5kg sugar*

Scrub the oranges and put in a preserving pan with the lemon juice and water. If the oranges bob to the top, put in an old plate to keep them below the water level. Bring to the boil, cover and put in the simmering oven for 4-5 hours or overnight.

Remove the pan from the oven. Scoop out the oranges and allow them to cool enough to handle. Cut in half, scoop out the flesh and the pips and return them to the liquid. Bring the orange liquid to the boil and boil with the lid off for 5 minutes. Strain through a sieve squeezing out all the juices.

Cut up the orange peel as fine or coarse as you like. Put half the prepared peel into the preserving pan along with half the strained liquid and 3 lb/1.25kg sugar. Place on the simmering plate and stir until all the sugar is dissolved.

Move to the boiling plate, and after boiling rapidly for 10-15 minutes, test for a setting point. When this point is reached, allow the marmalade to sit for 10 minutes so that the peel will not rise to the top in the jars. Pour into warm, sterilised jars, seal and label as for jam. Repeat with the remaining ingredients.

**Makes about 10 lb/4.5kg.**

..........................................................

# INDIAN CHUTNEY

······················································

This recipe has been a firm favourite in our family for many years. I am not sure of the origin. It gives a rich, sweet chutney, lovely with cheese and cold meats.

*1 lb/450g apples – peeled, cored and chopped*
*1 lb/450g onions – peeled and chopped*
*1 lb/450g ripe tomatoes*
*1 lb/450g raisins*
*1 lb/450g sultanas*
*1 lb/450g brown sugar*
*1 tsp ground ginger*
*1 tsp cayenne pepper*
*1¹/₂ tsp fresh curry powder*
*2 oz/50g salt*
*³/₄ pint/450ml malt vinegar*

Mix the spices with some of the vinegar. Put all the ingredients in a large pan, stand on the simmering plate and heat, stirring, until the sugar is dissolved and the mixture is boiling. Transfer to the simmering oven and cook until the vegetables are soft – about 1-1¹/₂ hours. Return to the simmering plate and boil slowly until the mixture is thick and brown. Pour into warm, sterilized jars.

**Makes about 6 lb/2.75kg.**
······················································

# LEMON AND LIME CHUTNEY

A chutney to serve with curries, it is best to make this when lemons or limes are on special offer in the shops. It needs to mature for at least a month after making, but it gets better with keeping.

*4 lb/1.8kg lemons and/or limes*
*2 lb/900g onions*
*2 oz/50g salt*
*¹/₂ oz/12g cardamom pods*
*¹/₂ oz/12g coriander seeds*
*2 pints/1200ml white wine vinegar*
*2 oz/50g green chillies – chopped*
*4 oz/100g fresh ginger – grated*
*3 lb/1.35kg sugar*

Slice the fruit and remove the pips. Put into a large bowl with the salt and the finely sliced onions. Tie the spices together in a muslin bag and add to the bowl along with the vinegar. Cover and leave to stand for 8 hours or overnight. Pour the mixture into a heavy-based preserving pan, add the chilli and ginger. Bring to the boil on the simmering plate, cover and place in the simmering oven for 1-1¹/₂ hours until the fruit and onions are softened.

Return the pan to the simmering plate and add the sugar, stirring constantly to dissolve the sugar. Transfer to the boiling plate and boil fast for 15-20 minutes. Stir frequently to prevent burning – it is a good idea to wear an oven gauntlet to protect your hand from splashes. It may be sufficient to have the pan half on the plate and still keep a good boil. Boil to reduce the liquid and make a thickish consistency – it will also thicken as it cools.

Remove the spice bag. Ladle the chutney into warm, clean, sterilised jars. Cover and seal while hot. Keep for at least one month in a cool, dark place before opening.

**Makes about 8lb/3.5kg.**

# SUGAR-FREE MINCEMEAT

I developed this recipe for my mother when she became a diabetic, and I felt she should not miss out on festive treats. I used it with puff pastry, to make mincemeat slices. With all the dried fruits in mincemeat there is no need for sugar, and to prevent fermentation I put the mixture in the simmering oven for 4-5 hours. The mincemeat will keep for at least 12 months, if there is any left. Make enough to wrap decoratively for presents and for use during the year. Mincemeat is a wonderful stuffing for baked apples.

*1 lb/450g cooking apples, peeled, cored and coarsely grated*
*8 oz/225g shredded suet or vegetarian substitute*
*12 oz/350g raisins*
*12 oz/350g sultanas*
*12 oz/350g currants*
*grated rind and juice of 2 oranges*
*grated rind and juice of 2 lemons*
*2 oz/50g slivered almonds*
*4 tsp mixed spice*
*1 tsp ground cinnamon*
*¹/₂ grated nutmeg*
*6 tbsp brandy*

Mix together all the ingredients except the brandy. Mix very thoroughly; I get the family to make this on a wet autumn afternoon and everyone has a good stir. Cover with a plate or a cloth and leave for at least 12 hours in a cool place. Stir again. Put the oven shelf on the floor of the simmering oven and put in the bowl of mincemeat, covered. Leave for 4-5 hours. Remove and set aside until cold. Stir in the brandy. Spoon into clean dry jars. Cover with wax discs, seal and label.

Makes about 5 lb/2.25kg.

# INDEX

# ACKNOWLEDGEMENTS

At the end of this labour of love I have to acknowledge with thanks a few of the many people who have helped along the way with this book: my good friend and help-mate during my Aga workshop days, Jane Frere, who persuaded me – no nagged me – into doing this book; Jon Croft and staff at Absolute Press for their confidence in me; everyone at the Aga Shop, Bath, for introducing me to so many interesting customers, who persuaded me to put pen to paper; Anne Coleborn who managed to decipher my writing and typed the manuscript so clearly; my husband Geoff and children Hanna, Dominic and Hugo who put up with lack of attention and un-balanced meals during recipe testing; and especially to my late mother, who cooked so well and with such love and care that she inspired me to make cooking and Home Economics my career.